KU-310-230

The London Market Guide

Andrew Kershman

The London Market Guide
Written by Andrew Kershman
Photographs by Andrew Kershman
Maps designed by Lesley Gilmour
Illustrations by Sebastian Airey
Book design by Susi Koch and Lesley Gilmour
Edited by David Gluck

All rights reserved. No part of this publication may be reproduced, stored in a retrieval system or transmitted in any form or by any means electronic, mechanical, photocopying, recording or otherwise without the prior consent of the publishers and copyright owners. Every effort has been made to ensure the accuracy of this book; however, due to the nature of the subject the publishers cannot accept responsibility for any errors which occur, or their consequences.

Published in 2008 by
Metro Publications
PO Box 6336
London
N1 6PY

Printed in India

© 2008 Andrew Kershman
British Library Cataloguing in Publication Data.
A catalogue record for this book is available from the British Library.

ISBN: 978-1-902910-30-7

In memory of my Mum, Joy Wright
(1931-2007)

Acknowledgements

My thanks go to all the stall holders who patiently answered my questions and even agreed to pose for a photograph. My editor, Paul Gluck, deserves special praise for his efforts particularly towards the end, when last minute changes and corrections where made. Lesley Gilmour also merits a special mention for her sterling work on the maps and illustrations for the book. My thanks also go to Susi Koch whose support and hard work have helped make this book possible.

Contents

How to use this book

market name

icons (see key on page 4)

area

map

market name

nearest transport

opening times

review

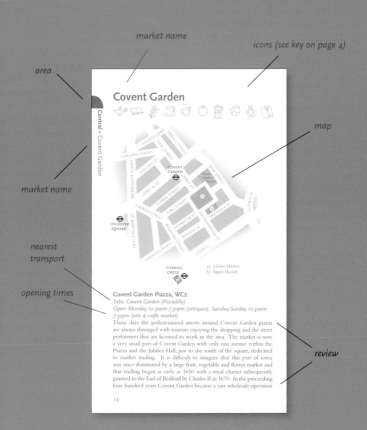

Covent Garden

Central · Covent Garden

a) Jubilee Market
b) Apple Market

Covent Garden Piazza, WC2
Tube: Covent Garden (Piccadilly)
Open: Monday 10:30am-7:30pm (antiques), Tuesday-Sunday 10:30am-7:30pm (arts & crafts market)

These days the pedestrianised streets around Covent Garden piazza are always thronged with tourists enjoying the shopping and the street performers that are licensed to work in the area. The market is now a very small part of Covent Garden with only one avenue within the Piazza and the Jubilee Hall, just to the south of the square, dedicated to market trading. It is difficult to imagine that this part of town was once dominated by a large fruit, vegetable and flower market and that trading began as early as 1656 with a royal charter subsequently granted to the Earl of Bedford by Charles II in 1670. In the proceeding four hundred years Covent Garden became a vast wholesale operation

14

Introduction

The London Market Guide has been chronicling the changes in London's markets for over 15 years and it is now hard for the author to visit a market without subsequently writing about how it has changed and what has disappeared. I have tried to avoid lapsing into reminiscence, my purpose is to tell you what markets are like today, but I hope you will forgive the occasional mention of a favourite café that has now closed or a stall holder that is no longer there.

Part of the difficulty in writing about London's street markets is that they are constantly changing and this is partly why they are so interesting. Brick Lane Market is a great example of this, with the itinerant traders that sell bric-à-brac from blankets constantly moving their location while more permanent changes have taken place with the success of the Sunday Upmarket and Backyard Market which have greatly added to the appeal of the market. Every visit brings new surprises and memorable experiences – when was the last time you had a memorable experience at a dull and reliable supermarket…

There have been some really encouraging changes in the market landscape of London in recent years. It is a real joy to visit Hackney's Broadway Market that has emerged from years of decline to become a vibrant and exciting place to shop on a Saturday. Another good news story is the growing popularity of North Cross Street Market that has blossomed in the last few years and now offers locals the chance to buy antiques and retro clothing along with essentials like fresh meat and fish. Both these markets are thriving by catering to the prosperous class of Londoners that regard shopping as a leisure activity rather than a chore. London's farmers markets have also continued to thrive, providing Londoners with quality fresh produce and also giving British farmers a vital means to sell directly to the public.

London's street markets are as varied as the capital itself. The South Bank Book Market feels like it belongs on the banks of the Seine, while Ridley Road is sometimes like a Jamaican street market with delicacies like goat meat and pigs extremities all on display and reggae playing loudly from the music stalls. Portobello and Camden Markets are magnets for tourists from around the world and have acquired an international character with German backpackers rubbing shoulders with Spanish punks as they go about their business. Whichever markets you choose to visit, I hope you enjoy the experience and find a few bargains along the way.

Brick Lane

Icon Index

antiques

books

fruit & veg

cut flower & plants

cloth

fresh fish

towels & bedding

fresh bread

pubs

fresh coffee

produce

hardware

arts & crafts

clothing

shoes

household goods

fresh meat

furniture

cafés & restaurants

bric-a-brac

music (CD's etc)

electrical goods

toys

toiletries

pet supplies

haberdashery

Central

Berwick & Rupert Street

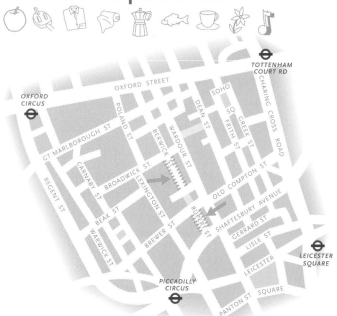

Berwick St, from Broadwick St extending south onto Rupert St, W1

Tube: Oxford Circus (Victoria, Central), Piccadilly Circus (Bakerloo, Piccadilly), Tottenham Court Road (Northern)
Open: Monday-Saturday 9am-5pm

Berwick Street is one of those special places that seem to capture something of the flavour of London and its people. There's been a fruit and veg market here since the 1840's but the traditional three story buildings that give the street its charm are now overshadowed by larger more recent developments. The 1960s supermarket and tower block at the junction with Peter Street are ugly but familiar while the recently office block at the junction with Broadwick Street is a glamorous construction of steel and glass. The market rumbles on as further building work continues, but one gets the feeling the market is tolerated rather than encouraged by Westminster Council.

Berwick Street market is a one-off because it is essentially a local market dealing in fruit and veg, but situated bang in the heart of London's Soho. Despite being restricted to the west side of the street and a gradual decline in the number of stalls, the market is still a wonderful place to shop with just about every fruit, vegetable and herb you could possibly need from the humble potato to Chinese black mushrooms and cassava. If you're looking for a particular delicacy the traders are always willing to point you to the right stall. More basic fruit and veg is often sold very cheaply with large bags of bananas, oranges or mushrooms going for £1, although it is a sensible idea to check the quality of the goods before buying. The produce is still very good, but the elaborate displays of fruit and veg that were once a feature of the Peter Street end of the market are a thing of the past.

Supplementing the fruit and veg stalls is the long-established and excellent fishmonger. Ian Keene has been selling fish – collected each day from Billingsgate – at Berwick Street for over 40 years and continues to trade with stoic determination despite the disappearance of the complimentary cheese and bread stalls. The largest and most established fruit and veg stall occupies a central place in the market and is run with characteristic zeal by the the old geezer who still manages to call out his special offers, regardless of the lack of competition these days. Ronnie's flower stall is going strong and makes a colourful display in the centre of Berwick Street and he is joined by a number of more recent additions to the market selling household and small electrical goods, a very well organised CD and DVD stall and a stall specialising in herbs, dried fruits and nuts. There are usually a few clothing and accessory stalls on the market but these are less regular features of Berwick Street.

By walking south across Peter Street and through the narrow pedestrian Walker's Court (with porno outlets on either side), Rupert Street market can be reached. This market used to have some fruit and veg stalls, but they have gone in the last few years leaving a handful of traders selling bags, belts and cheap new clothing. Amid all the combat clothing and novelty T-shirts there were one or two interesting things, but generally speaking Rupert Street is now a very small and run-down market. On my last visit on a cloudy Monday afternoon the street was empty of stalls and I instead turned my attention to *Cheapo Cheapo Records* (53 Rupert Street) which is one of London's best discount music shops and well worth a visit.

Anyone who loves London's markets must harbour some resentment towards Westminster Council for the changes in recent years, but the development of inner city supermarkets has also taken its toll and traders now claim the congestion charge is making matters even worse. Despite all the problems Berwick Street still has a unique atmosphere and is well worth a visit if you're in the centre of town and looking for something a little more interesting than the shopping hoards of Oxford Street.

Berwick Street Market

Refreshment

The number and variety of eating places on Berwick Street has greatly increased in recent years. *Bar Du Marché* and *The Mediterranean Café* are both at the Broadwick Street end of the market, as is the trendy *Beatroot* vegetarian café and a long established fish and chip restaurant. A recent arrival to the street is the *Flat White Expresso Bar* which is as trendy as the name might suggests.

Local Attractions

Berwick Street is also a good place to look for fabric sold by the metre with lots of shops including *Borovick Fabric* and *Soho Silks*. For those interested in cutting edge music, there are also numerous trendy vinyl stores along Berwick Street, but these are not places to visit if you are looking for the latest Justin Timberlake track, although *Rough Trade* is a little more mainstream.

Getting a Stall

For further details about a stall at either Berwick or Rupert Street contact Westminster City Council (see appendix).

Cabbages & Frocks

St Marylebone Parish Church, Marylebone High Street, W1

www.cabbagesandfrocks.co.uk
Tube: Baker Street
Open: Saturday 11am-5pm

Cabbages & Frocks is a brave attempt to establish a new and vibrant market in London when so many have closed down in recent years. It is the only market not to be named after the area in which it is located, indicating that this is a rethink of what people want from a market in the 21st century with an emphasis upon quality, originality and fun rather than shopping for the basics. The market started life in Hampstead before moving to the beautiful courtyard of *St Marylebone Parish Church* in the summer of 2006. In this new location as many as forty stalls can trade, offering a fine choice of prepared foods, clothing and accessories as well as occasional items for the home.

The organisers go to some effort to make the market attractive with white canvas covered stalls arranged around the church's vast horse chestnut tree and several large banners advertising the market to passing pedestrians. The food stalls are very good with one trader specialising in food from the Algarve including large slices of tortilla and delicious fish cakes, while its neighbour had a good selection of fresh pastries and another offered a choice of homemade cupcakes. One stall was doing a roaring trade in handmade chocolates with lots of unusual creations like spicy ginger covered in chocolate for a very reasonable £4 a box. Another busy stall offers its own brand of bath soaks and skin creams made from natural ingredients and sold in attractive boxed sets for £15. On a recent visit there were several stalls offering reasonably priced designer jewellery with one selling original lacework accessories handmade in Turkey with unusual rings for only £9. For those more interested in frocks than cabbages, there are several stalls selling discounted nearly new designer wear and accessories with one offering a hardly worn Channel dress for just £80 and a pair of D&G sunglasses for the bargain price of £35. Several milliners proudly displayed their wares – my favourite being the 1930s inspired ladies felt hats in a variety of colours for just £45 each. One of the most unusual traders at the market had travelled from Norfolk with their selection of vintage fabrics, cushions, throws, tableware and small items of furniture which were all carefully displayed and clearly priced.

Cabbages and Frocks is a wonderful and imaginative venture and a welcome addition to the market scene of London. The organisers are always seeking new ways to promote the market and have regular themed days and special events to help keep things interesting. Anyone who regrets the decline in London's street markets will get a boost from visiting this market on a busy summer day.

Refreshment

The market has several stalls selling fresh salads and other take-away goodies and the coffee stall does a mean cappuccino. Marylebone High Street has lots of good cafés including the wonderful but expensive *Café Valerie*.

Local Attractions

If you like second-hand shopping Marylebone High Street has many good charity shops. The fabulous *Wallace Collection* is just around the corner on Manchester Square.

Getting a Stall

For further details phone 020 7794 1636 or send an e-mail to info@cabbagesandfrocks.co.uk.

Charing Cross Collector's Fair

Under Charing Cross Arches, WC2
(end of Northumberland Avenue)

Tube: Embankment (Northern, Bakerloo, District and Circle)
Charing Cross (Northern, Jubilee and Bakerloo)
Rail: Charing Cross
Open: Saturday 8.30am-1pm

Every Saturday hundreds of collectors congregate in this unprepossessing underground car park in central London. Among the thirty or so stalls are specialists in military medals, coins, stamps, bank notes, postcards, cigarette cards and even phone cards. Collecting things can seem to the uninitiated a dull, rather unexciting pastime and the initial impression when entering this concrete bunker will probably confirm this view. The average age of those attending is about fifty, they are nearly all male and a very great number sport beards of some description – often in conjunction with a cardigan of grey or brown hue. A brief wander among the stalls, however, is sure to unearth something of interest. The coins on display are a good first stop because of their intrinsic appeal. The neatly written labels give details of the type and age of the coin and the dealer is usually willing to expound at length if you want to know more. I was surprised that some coins of considerable antiquity

11

were so cheap. An English half groat dating from 1461 could be bought here for £16, a Roman denarius for £23 and a Syrian coin from 142 BC for only £12. Other coins of various denominations and ages were piled in great heaps for only a few pence each. It is here that I discovered that my only family heirloom (a 1965 coin commemorating Winston Churchill) was worth the princely sum of 60p. Not all the coins here are cheap and some serious collectors spend a good deal of money at the market. I witnessed a visitor paying over £1,000 for a boxed set of three coins.

There are many stamp dealers here and experienced collectors spend some time pawing the catalogues with a magnifying glass and tweezers looking for something to add to their collection. It is possible to start a collection for only a few pence but in some instances whole collections are for sale. I asked one bearded, cardigan-clad, stall-holder the value of his most expensive stamp, but my question was clearly a crass one for his brow creased as he explained that he didn't think about his collection in that way and then generously volunteered the figure of £75 to help me.

The postcard stalls are a little more accessible to the first-time visitor. They are usually arranged by country or area, but in some cases by subject and are fascinating not only for the aging pictures on the front but often for the handwritten messages found on the back, addressed to long deceased correspondents. The political postcards are interesting, one card commemorated the Locarno Conference of 1925 with pictures of the participants including a young Mussolini, while another French postcard used a cartoon to lambaste Prussian Imperialism. Although not a collector, I was tempted by the notion of owning a little bit of history for only a few pounds.

Charing Cross Collectors' Fair is a fascinating place to visit and a real culture shock for anyone unfamiliar with the fusty and arcane world of collecting. The market is fairly busy each week, but most of the visitors are regulars and one stall holder complained that he rarely sees a new face here on a Saturday. Rodney runs the market and plans to retire in a few years which may put an end to this unique London event. I enjoyed my visit and left with six beautiful Swiss postcards depicting flowers in my pocket which cost only £3.50 and can be added to my now much devalued heirloom.

Charing Cross Collector's Fair

Refreshment
The Collectors' Fair is located in the centre of town and is surrounded by cafés, restaurants and pubs. My favourite is the café in the Embankment Garden which is just the other side of Charing Cross Station.

Local Attractions
There are many places to visit after a morning at the Collectors' Fair, including *The National Portrait Gallery*, *The National Gallery* and *The Southbank Centre* which always has a busy programme of events and concerts and also features a great book market under Waterloo Bridge (see page 32). *The Embankment Gardens* extend along the north bank of the Thames and are wonderful places to visit when the weather is fine.

Getting a Stall
For further details contact the market manager on 01483 281 771.

Covent Garden

a) Jubilee Market
b) Apple Market

Covent Garden Piazza, WC2

Tube: Covent Garden (Piccadilly)
Open: Monday 10.30am-7.30pm (antiques), Tuesday-Sunday 10.30am-7.30pm (arts & crafts market)

These days the pedestrianised streets around Covent Garden piazza are always thronged with tourists enjoying the shopping and the street performers that are licensed to work in the area. The market is now a very small part of Covent Garden with only one avenue within the Piazza and the Jubilee Hall, just to the south of the square, dedicated to market trading. It is difficult to imagine that this part of town was once dominated by a large fruit, vegetable and flower market and that trading began as early as 1656 with a royal charter subsequently granted to the Earl of Bedford by Charles II in 1670. In the proceeding four hundred years Covent Garden became a vast wholesale operation with its famous porters providing a bit of working-class culture amid the increasingly retail and office environment of the West End. All this changed in 1973 when the wholesale market moved to a modern purpose built site at Nine Elms (see page 120) and by 1980 Covent Garden was transformed into the tourist oriented crafts and antiques market we recognise today. For some time the market extended over three sites but the Opera House Market to the north was closed when the *Royal Opera House* was redeveloped in the mid 90s.

Apple Market

Designed by Charles Fowler in 1830, Covent Garden Piazza is a cheerful apple-red and vanilla coloured structure housing two floors of (mainly High Street) shops interspersed with glass covered arcades. Until 1973 this building was dedicated to market trade, but these days the Apple Market is just a small part of the Piazza – occupying one corner with about 50 stalls selling antiques and collectables on Mondays and arts and crafts during the rest of the week. There are some lovely pieces of artwork and crafts available here with jewellery, wooden toys, clocks, clothing and accessories all well presented and commanding high prices. Recent offerings included colourful hand-dyed scarves for £10, quality leather bags for £30 and brightly coloured girl's dresses reduced from £25 to a very reasonable £17. The crafts market has quite a few jewellery designers selling their contemporary creations and many of them accepting individual commissions if customers want a bespoke item.

There are so many tourists passing through the market on any day of the week that the stalls are highly prized and the people that trade from them are organised and professional with careful displays and many dealers accepting credit cards. The Monday antiques and collectables market has an unusual mix of stalls with one trader specialising in old vinyl and pop magazines from the 1950s onwards while another displayed a small number of genuine antiques with several china plates dating from 1890 for £10 each. Most of the antique and collectable stalls trade from the Jubilee Hall on a Monday, but there are always enough interesting things here to make it worth visiting. Recently I found a very unusual bronze neckless dating from the 1960s which was worth its asking price of £25 and could probably be bought for a little less with a bit of judicial haggling. There are several stalls situated at eastern side of the Piazza (facing the *London Transport Museum*) selling among other things sweets, framed photos of London and scented soaps.

Jubilee Market

This part of the market is much larger than the Apple Market, but the building is less attractive and the items for sale tend to be a little more tourist orientated with small pub signs, heraldic symbols and union jack T-shirts all on display during the week. There are usually a few astrology and palm reading stalls and for those looking for sustenance of a more mundane nature there are several food stalls offering things like smoothies and sandwiches at a reasonable price. As well as the novelty items there are also a few stalls offering practical things like cheap bags and street fashion which are worth a look. This part of Covent Garden is really at its best on Mondays when the majority of the antique and collectable stalls set up here, offering anything from piles of junk jewellery for £1 an item to attractive displays of genuine collectables such as a small chess board with a complete set of very fine pieces for the hefty price tag of £125. There were several stalls selling kitchen collectables such as a 1940s milk jug for £15 and a good condition Royal Doulton plate from the 1950s for a very reasonable £16. The Jubilee Hall is a popular feature of London's antiques business with several traders from Bermondsey and Camden Passage also trading here on a Monday. The place is well worth a visit if your in search of an unusual gift or just want to enjoy the quirky atmosphere with lots of regulars showing up here to pass the time and occasionally haggle over a particular item that has caught their fancy. Take a few minutes to look at the plaque on the side of Jubilee Hall, on the corner of Southampton Street, which gives a brief account of the market's illustrious past.

Local Attractions

There are numerous attractions in and around Covent Garden the most prominent being *The London Transport Museum* (right next to the market). Street performers are a popular feature of Covent Garden with acrobats, dancers and opera singers plying their trade. Those interested in architecture should take a look at *St Paul's Church* to the west of the Piazza which was designed by Inigo Jones. Just ten minutes walk away, on Trafalgar Square, is *The National Gallery* and *The National Portrait Gallery.*

Getting a Stall

For a stall at the arts and crafts market phone 020 7836 9136 or e-mail: info@coventgardenmarket.co.uk.

For a stall at the antiques market contact *Sherman and Waterman Associates Ltd* who can be reached on 020 7240 7405.

Covent Garden

Earlham Street

Earlham Street between Shaftesbury Avenue and Seven Dials, WC2

Tube: Leicester Square (Northern and Piccadilly); Covent Garden (Piccadilly)
Open: Monday-Saturday 11am-7.30pm

Earlham Street Market was once an all purpose market providing all kinds of essentials for the local community. The last fruit and veg stall left the market about ten years ago and the five or six stalls that remain now deal in street fashion with several flower sellers at the Seven Dials end of the street offering elegant cut flowers. This might sound uninspiring but the clothing stalls offer a good choice in seasonal street fashion with a particularly good selection of T-shirts with comic or iconic images on them and usually a few unusual items such as fur lined sheep skin boots recently on sale for just £10. The cut flower stalls are not cheap but do offer a much more interesting range of flora than you find at most market flower stalls. The street has a number of interesting small shops including a traditional hardware store and on the corner of Shaftesbury Avenue the only London branch of *Fopp* which sells cheap books, music and DVDs. There have been a few regrettable closures on the street with the traditional butchers shutting after several hundred years of trading and the fabulous *Oxfam Original* store also closing down. Earlham Street is not worth going out of your way to visit, but is well worth taking a look at if you're in the West End.

Earlham Street

Refreshments

There is a basic caff and a mediterranean take-away food stall on the street and just around the corner is the excellent *Monmouth Coffee Shop* for a reviving cup of Java.

Getting a Stall

Contact Camden Council (see appendix).

Leadenhall

Whittington Avenue, EC3
(off Gracechurch Street & Leadenhall Street)

Tube: Bank (Central and Northern), Monument (Circle and District)
Open: Monday-Friday 7am-4pm

Leadenhall has been the site of a market for nearly six hundred years and in that time has twice been destroyed by fire and rebuilt. The grand cast-iron and stone structure that stands today was designed by Sir Horace Jones in 1881 and has a wonderful atmosphere with arched thoroughfares leading to a domed central meeting place. The only hitch in this tale of continuity is the fact that Leadenhall market has evolved to the stage where it is not a market at all, but rather a permanent shopping arcade containing many High Street shops including a branch of Jigsaw and Waterstones. It is still an interesting place to visit and there are several very fine greengrocers, fishmongers and butchers within the arcade which continue to sell the kind of produce that has been sold here for centuries.

Another thing that gives this market a unique character is its location in the heart of London's financial square mile with Richard Rodgers' Lloyds' building looming above it. From Leadenhall Place you can enjoy the sight of people going up and down in the external glass lifts of this spectacular structure of steel and glass. If you don't enjoy crowds it's advisable to avoid this area during lunchtime when thousands of city folk in suits descend upon the market to get something to eat or do a bit of shopping. Leadenhall is an interesting place to visit on any weekday but is at its best in the weeks running up to Christmas when the food shops are festooned with seasonal fare.

Leather Lane

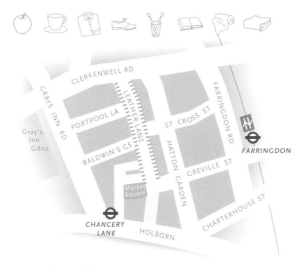

Leather Lane, EC1
(between Clerkenwell Road and Greville Street)

Tube: Farringdon (Circle and Metropolitan), Chancery Lane (Central)
Open: Monday-Friday 10.30am-2.00pm

Leather Lane is the last major market in the Clerkenwell area. Exmouth Market once rivalled its neighbour but has declined into a much smaller food market, while Farringdon Book Market closed in the 1990s when the last remaining bookseller retired. Leather Lane has survived by becoming a lunch time market catering for the office workers of the area rather than Clerkenwell's declining residential population. It's a functional weekday market, but is still great fun and well worth visiting even if you're not a nine-to-fiver. To avoid the crowds, it's advisable to visit the market between 10.30am and 12 noon – before the street fills with people out for a quick shop during their lunch break. The cheap magazine stall on the corner of Clerkenwell Road is a good place to start, with hundreds of slightly out of date mags covering anything from bodybuilding to celebrity gossip for 80p each or 3 for £2. There is also a very good fruit and veg stall here selling the basics as well as more fancy stuff like mange tout and fresh herbs. There are numerous clothes stalls along Leather Lane with lots of seasonal casual and office gear to be found for under £10 and discount rails where end-of-lines are sold for a fiver. On a recent visit one stall reduced all their ladies wear to £3 and acquired a rabid crowd of shoppers jostling each other for a bargain. One of the best stalls at this end of the market is the shoe seller where reasonable quality men's and women's shoes are sold for £15-25 a pair.

Further south, between Portpool Lane and St Cross Street, are some of the most interesting stalls including the deli trader stocking some of the fine foods that could once have been bought from the gone but not forgotten Ferraro Continental Food Store. The market changes depending on the season with body warmers and winter jackets giving way to colourful T-shirts, swimwear and sandals as summer comes around. Just opposite the junction with St Cross Street is Camden Age Concern – one of the best charity shops in London and well worth a visit if you're a bargain hunter. The fabric stall nearby represents excellent value with some large remnants for only a fiver and many cotton fabrics for just £2 per metre. Also in this part of the market is a very good flower and plant stall with a reasonable choice of floral bargains including on a recent visit some very healthy looking Camellia plants just coming into flower for only £6.50.

Further along, Leather Lane has one of the best jewellery stalls in London with simple rings for as little as £5. One customer asked for arm bracelets and from behind the stall emerged a box with a variety of funky designs to choose from. Another regular trader who deserves special mention is the bedding and towel man who offers two white pillow cases and a kingsize duvet with an attractive embroidered pattern for only £30 and two large cotton bath towels for only £10.

Further south there are numerous stalls selling clothing, shoes, toiletries and funky jewellery. Leather Lane is always busy at lunch times, but few tourists make their way here and this keeps the prices very low with busy office workers unwilling to spend their hard earned cash on anything that isn't very good value. Recently I found nylon rucksacks for £5 at Leather Lane that were as much as £10 in some West End street markets.

The end of the market is marked by a square of stalls between Beauchamp Gardens and Greville Street. This part of the is not always busy and on recent visits there have been several empty spaces. The traders that do show up here regularly are worth checking out with the DVD stall offering some good deals on recent releases and the trader selling discounted biscuits and other food stuffs always busy. There are usually a few people selling discounted smart ladies wear and the shoe stall in the far corner offers a reasonable selection of ladies shoes for around £30.

Leather Lane

Refreshment

Leather Lane has lots of good places to eat and drink. There are several stalls on the market offering good quality take-away food with *Daddy Donkey Mexican Grill* and *Sunny's Olive Tree* both very busy at lunch time. For tasty food in a more traditional environment, *The Bagel Bakery* and *The Traditional Plaice* fish and chip shop are both old favourites. *The Mediterranean Food Bar* and *Le Panini* are popular cafés and do a decent cappuccino. *Farina's Café and Restaurant*, opposite Cross Street, is my favourite on the street offering traditional caff grub in a largely unaltered wood clad environment.

Local Attractions

There are numerous interesting shops in the area. *L. Terroni & Sons*, just opposite the market on Clerkenwell, is still one of the best Italian deli's in town and one of the last vestiges of Clerkenwell's Italian community. Although the market offers very little in the way of literature, *Soho Original Bookshop* carries a good range of discounted books. *The Sir John Soane's Museum* (13 Lincoln's Inn Fields, WC2) is one of the most unusual museums in London and is within walking distance of the market.

Getting a Stall

For further details contact Camden Council (see appendix).

Lower Marsh

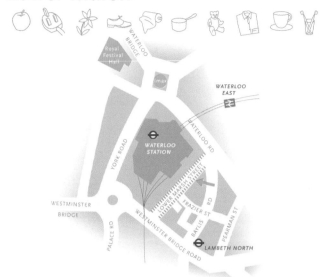

Lower Marsh from Westminster Bridge Road to Baylis Road, SE1

Tube: Waterloo (Northern, Bakerloo, Waterloo & City),
Lambeth North (Bakerloo)
Rail: Waterloo (take the exit nearest Platform 1, follow the road down
and take the underpass into Leake Street)
Open: Monday-Friday from around 9am, with market fully operational
over lunch time: 11am-2pm; some stall-holders also set up on Saturdays,
but the market is a lot more patchy

Having been forcibly down-sized by the demise of the GLC in the
eighties (which knocked out a considerable chunk of its lunch time
trade), Lower Marsh is no longer the large, vibrant market of former
times when it stretched right into The Cut. The white markings on
the tarmac where stalls formerly traded are testament to the market's
decline. Despite this downturn, traders on this site have over 150 years of
tradition to uphold and a reliable influx of shoppers still passes through
the street on a weekday. As with most community markets, utility is the
name of the game at Lower Marsh with traders focusing on everyday
needs: fruit and veg, household goods and kitchen equipment (check
out the deals on pan sets and knives), toiletries, luggage, haberdashery
and fabric. Underwear and socks, bedding plants and flowers, sweets,
cards, batteries, women's office wear, shoes, hair accessories, CDs,

Lower Marsh

bedding and towels all get a look in too. The cheap office outfits where great value with most items sold for only £3 and a few summer skirts sold for only £2. The shoe stall was equally good value with a limited selection of footwear for £5 a pair. By far the best thing about Lower Marsh Street Market is the fruit and veg stall which has been run by Mani for many years and sells a wonderful selection of fresh seasonal fruit and veg from everyday produce like Bramley apples to more unusual things like celeriac and fresh watercress. Mani supplies many of the capital's best restaurants and his stall is well worth visiting if you're in the area – his stall is usually found just outside the Crockatt and Powell Bookshop. The street itself is probably more of a pull than the market with a lively blend of trendy boutiques, specialist businesses and traditional shops.

Refreshment

When it comes to eating, Lower Marsh has lots to offer the visitor. Food stops mirror the hybrid mix of shops, with *Marie's Café* acting as a greasy spoon during the day and becoming a Thai diner at night. The most interesting café on the street is *Scooter Works* which, as the name suggests, started life as a Lambretta workshop that sold coffee on the side and is now a café with Lambrettas used for decoration. For a healthy lunch *Coopers Natural Foods* has a good selection of wholefood and vegetarian options. If you scoff at the idea of health food and would prefer a liquid lunch, try *Cubana* at the Waterloo Road end of the market, or the very trendy *Camel & Artichoke* in the middle of Lower Marsh. Further afield on Cornwall Road, 'bespoke bakery' *Konditor & Cook* is crammed with lovingly-crafted cakes, breads and sandwiches and also has a concession in the *Young Vic* on The Cut if you fancy a sit-down treat.

Local Attractions

Clothing is one of Lower Marsh's fortes, with a number of both new and vintage shops; try retro boutique *Radio Days* for impeccably suave clothes, furniture and ephemera and *What The Butler Wore* for racks full of stylishly 50s-70s clothes. Other interesting shops include the classical music shop, *Gramex*, and the *Far East Supermarket*, which stocks everything from pak choi to tom yum, as well as great spices and strange packets of things like *Great Impression* 'losing weight' tea. Those of a literary leaning should not miss *Jane Gibberd Secondhand Books* (20 Lower Marsh) which is a beautiful little shop and the new independent bookshop, *Crockatt & Powell* – just opposite. Further afield there is plenty to explore, with Lower Marsh within easy walking distance of the *Southbank Centre* which includes the *Hayward Gallery*, the *NFT*, and the *London Eye*. The massive *IMAX 3-D Cinema* is also just around the corner.

Getting a Stall

For further details contact Lambeth Council (see appendix).

Piccadilly Market

St James's Churchyard, Piccadilly, W1
www.st-james-piccadilly.org/market.html
Tube: Piccadilly Circus (Piccadilly, Bakerloo)
Open: Tuesday 10am-6pm (antiques),
Wednesday-Saturday 10am-6pm (arts & crafts)

Piccadilly is a four-lane road which is always crammed with heavy traffic and its pavements are equally busy with pedestrians. The courtyard of St James' Church is a welcome quiet space amid all the chaos and is the perfect site for this arts and crafts and antiques market. The large wrought iron gates of the church are covered with ivy and act as an effective barrier between the street and the shade of the courtyard. When you enter it's worth looking down to notice the heavy flagstones that cover the floor, quite a few of which still bear inscriptions in memory of those long departed. Look up and there is the spire of this fine Wren church whose bells chime into life every hour.

On Tuesdays the market is given over to antiques, collectables and bric-à-brac with lots of small items to sift through including pens, paperweights, antique and second-hand books, pictures, stamps, coins, cigarette cards and old medals. The postcard stall is a great place to while away some time with lots of aged postcards to admire – some of which have been completed with accounts of holidays from many years past. The political postcards are particularly fascinating and represent a little piece of history often for less than a pound. The coins are also popular although many are just piled into boxes with browsers invited to sift through for something of interest. The market is a good place to find fine silverware with several stalls selling cutlery at reasonable prices. One stall offers larger items like clocks, wooden boxes and some very attractive watercolours for between £75 and £85. The stall selling old prints and maps is also a rewarding place to spend some time with a good selection of maps and prints of the Capital.

If collectables are not your cup of tea, the market is best visited between Wednesday and Saturday when it is given over to contemporary arts and crafts although a few souvenir stalls also take up residence here. The latter are easily identified, resplendent as they are with Union Jack T-shirts, and various models and pictures featuring London buses and red phone boxes. It is easy to sneer at such touristy stuff, but the visitors seem to like it and I still have my plastic Eiffel Tower from a visit to Paris in 1992. The stall selling bags and purses is reasonable value with leather bags for about £35-£50. Unlike the antiques market, the provenance of goods during the rest of the week is very broad, with a stall selling dolls, watches, badges and medals from Russia, another specialising in goods from Tibet and another selling Indian clothing largely made from cotton and in a style that might best be described as 'ethnic'. The watch stall has a more contemporary feel, with modern stainless steel watches from only £10. The scented soap stall is tucked away at the back of the market, but is easy to find by following the aroma that exudes from that corner. The leather bound notebooks are attractive and range in price from £5 to £30 for a large volume. One of my favourite stalls is situated at the opposite corner of the market and specialises in colourful modern glassware and jewellery with funky glass rings for only £12. The stall has quite a few devotees and on a recent visit a woman had made a special trip to pick up a few things for friends having visited the stall a few weeks previously. Those looking for a momento from their visit to the capital could do a lot worse than the stall selling framed contemporary photos of London which range in price from £7-£50.

St James's Market caters for the many tourists that visit the area, but is still a great place to visit – if only to escape from the crowds and enjoy some relative tranquillity in the church courtyard. The church itself is a fantastic example of Wren's work and is often open if you want to have a look inside. There are plans to redevelop the site in the coming years and this will involve the closure of the market for some time – check the market website before making a special trip to visit the market.

Piccadilly Market

Refreshment
There is a café attached to the annex of the church which is now run by the *Café Nero* chain. It's a great place to relax, particularly on fine days when there is seating outside. If you fancy going up-market *The Ritz* is about 5 minutes further west along Piccadilly and does a slap-up tea at a truly exorbitant price.

Local Attractions
Just a little further along Piccadilly is The Royal Academy of Arts which is a good place to while away a few hours. Piccadilly is becoming one of the main streets for bookshops in London and is the site for both the flagship Waterstones store and Hatchards. If you want to visit another market, proceed north up Regent Street and cut through Carnaby Street to Berwick Street Market which is still a great Soho institution (see page 6 for details).

Getting a Stall
If you are interested in having a stall at Piccadilly Market contact the Rector's office on 020 7734 4511 or visit the Rectory (in the courtyard of the church) during market hours.

Smithfield

Charterhouse Street, EC1

Tube: Farringdon and Barbican
(Circle, Metropolitan and Hammersmith and City)
Open: Monday-Friday 4am-12noon

Smithfield Market is the last wholesale market in London to remain on its original site. Meat has been sold here for over eight hundred years. The present building is an impressive edifice of iron, stone and brick, designed by Sir Horace Jones (who also designed Leadenhall Market) and built in 1866. Behind the immutable exterior, however, things have not stayed still and the market has undergone a £70 million redevelopment in recent years.

If you walk through the central archway at the bottom of St John Street and take a look down any of the buyers' avenues the change is easy to see. The interior of the massive Victorian building has been stripped out and, instead of the rather dark chaotic workings of the old market, new avenues have been created with each trader selling meat from modern counters and the meat being unpacked behind glass screens directly from the lorries. These changes were primarily introduced to improve efficiency and conform to hygiene regulations, but they also make this a far more welcoming place for members of the public to shop, if also diminishing some of the market's spit and sawdust vitality.

Early in the morning all the trade is on a large commercial scale, with wholesalers, butchers and buyers for London's restaurants and hotels doing their business. After about eight in the morning trade begins to slow down and those interested in making smaller purchases can be more easily served. I asked one trader whether he could sell one of his corn-fed chickens, rather than the box of eight that cost £20. His response was friendly and succinct "oh yeah, we always welcome RM", and when he noticed my look of incomprehension he kindly explained "RM means ready money". There are some excellent meaty bargains to be found here, making it a worthwhile destination if you have a large carnivorous family and a spacious freezer compartment. Among the bargains was a large box of frozen chicken legs (about thirty legs) for £7.50, while more unusual things like prepared stewing rabbit was only £3.50 per box. Another change in favour of retail customers is the increase in prepared meats and other things like Italian pannetone cakes being sold here. Smithfield is a pleasant and friendly place to shop in the morning and there are usually quite a few people strolling through the well-lit avenues looking for bargains.

Refreshment

There are lots of places to get refreshment in and around the market from early in the morning. Among the more established are *The Hope and Sir Loin* pub on St John Street (open from 6.30am) and the *Fox & Anchor* on Chamberhouse Street (open from 7am). There is also a *Coffee Republic* right on the corner of Cow Cross Street. Also on Cow Cross Street is an excellent veggie café called *The Greenway*, which is a welcome stop if you've had enough of meat for one morning.

Southbank Book Market

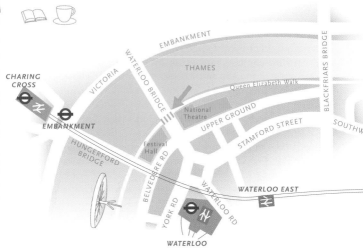

Riverside Walk under Waterloo Bridge in front of the NFT

Tube/Rail: Waterloo (Northern and Piccadilly)
Open: Daily noon-6pm (winter); 11am-7pm (summer)

It would be hard to imagine a more perfect location for a book market than on the south bank of the Thames, just outside the National Film Theatre (NFT), under the protection of Waterloo Bridge and with a fantastic view of the London skyline. Not only is it a good place to browse for books but, with a broad tree-lined pedestrian "boulevard", it also has a romantic atmosphere. I am not alone in thinking this – it was here that Hugh Grant made his declaration of love in the film *Four Weddings and a Funeral* and I know of one couple that carried out a good deal of their courtship here. The secret of the place is that, although it is in the centre of London, it's spirit and atmosphere is reminiscent of the banks of the Seine. After only a few minutes of browsing among the books I feel the urge to don a black polo neck, start smoking Gitanes and buy at least one book concerning existentialism.

The market has around sixty tables heaving under the weight of thousands of books covering most subjects. Works by all the giants of European and American literature can be found here including such names as Dickens, Balzac, Henry James, Orwell, Steinbeck and Kafka. If you prefer a good page turner there are enough books by the likes of Jilly Cooper, Joanna Trollop and Catherine Cookson to keep you entertained. This is also a good market to visit for academic and reference books with plenty of philosophy, psychology, art history and architecture. Naturally, being in the heart of the recently modernised *Southbank Centre* there is a good selection of plays, screenplays and books about film and theatre. Biographies are also well represented with anything from Kitty Kelly's prurient treatment of Frank Sinatra to more noble attempts to capture the lives of novelist Graham Greene or movie star Greta Garbo. There are also a few stalls selling mounted prints, usually illustrations taken from old books. The range of prints is fairly limited and a good deal of it consists of old maps, but there are sometimes things of interest to be uncovered.

The Southbank Book Market is not the cheapest place to find second-hand books, with most paperbacks selling for around half their new price, but among the thousands of books on offer you can usually find the odd bargain such as the paperback edition of Bertrand Russell's *History of Western Philosophy* I found recently for a mere £4. Anyway most of the people visiting here are really interested in enjoying the atmosphere and having a browse, rather than trying to save a few quid.

Refreshment

The *NFT* café is right next to the market, but the food is unexceptional and expensive. You might be better at the coffee bar just outside the *National Theatre*. Further west along the Thames are several cafés and restaurants housed within the Southbank Centre.

Local Attractions

The Southbank Centre has been recently modernised and now looks a lot smarter while still offering cutting-edge art exhibitions at the *Hayward Gallery*, classical and contemporary concerts and dance performances at the *Royal Festival* and *Queen Elizabeth Halls*, and art cinema and the annual *London Film Festival* at the *NFT*. The centre is also home to *Foyles* bookshop which is worth visiting if the market has not slated your appetite for books.

Getting a Stall

There are only ten licenses to sell books on this site, and the current traders have no plans to leave.

Southbank Book Market

Strutton Ground

Strutton Ground
(the south side of Victoria Street), SW1

Tube: St James's Park (Circle, District)
Open: Monday-Friday 11.30am-3pm

Strutton Ground is a small lunchtime market in the heart of Victoria. Every weekday around twenty stalls set up here and await the rush of office workers during the lunch hour. If you don't like crowds it's a good idea to visit this market either before 12 noon or after 2pm. The market offers high quality but basic fruit and veg, cut flowers, cheap DVDs and CDs, and good value women's office clothing with suits starting from £25.

Among the stalls was one doing a brisk business in womens' casual clothing, with all items for £6 and a crowd of office workers sifting through the rails for something in their size. There are several stalls selling fashionable shoes with one offering quality footwear for £5-£15 and the others selling a more limited range of disposable summer sandals for as little as a pound. There's also a stall dealing in branded cosmetics at well below High Street prices that is always popular with the regulars. There are several mixed stalls on the market with one selling underwear and sunglasses, and another stocking bags, belts and batteries at very reasonable prices. The jewellery stall is great value with a selection of traditional silver jewellery starting from £3.50 and going up to £15. A recent addition to the market is a stall selling nightclothes including Japanese style cotton bathrobes for only £12 and several nightdresses reduced to just a few quid to clear.

Refreshment

Being a lunchtime market, there are no end of places to get a drink or a bite to eat. Among the best are *The Trio Bar* for basic food, *The Strutton Arms* public house for a pint, *Greens* for take-away wholefood and *Stiles* bakery for traditional pastries and bread. At the top end of the market is the long established *Laughing Halibut* for traditional fish and chips as well as *The Express Coffee Co.* which does good coffee but is short on seating.

Local Attractions

There is no book stall on the market, but an *Oxfam Bookshop* has moved onto the street and offers a fantastic selection of second-hand books at reasonable prices. In terms of tourist attractions the *Houses of Parliament* and *Westminster Abbey* are within walking distance east along Victoria Street.

Getting a Stall

For further details contact Westminster Council (see appendix).

Tachbrook Street

Tachbrook Street between Warwick Way and Churton Street, SW1
Tube: Pimlico (Victoria), Victoria (Victoria, District and Circle)
Rail: Victoira
Open: Tuesday-Friday 9.30am-4.30pm, Saturday 9.30am-4.30pm
(some stalls)

Tachbrook Street Market has seen much better days in its long history dating back to the 19th century. It has now dwindled to just half a dozen stalls selling quality fruit and veg, cut flowers, bedding and towels as well as fresh bread. There have been some encouraging changes in recent years with the arrival of a stall specialising in olives and olive oil and a few dealing in second-hand furniture and knick-knacks, one of which had a good selection of costume jewellery at very reasonable prices. The market now boasts not one but two fishmongers which is a real rarity for any London market. Tachbrook Street is a charming little market and given the appeal of the nearby shops and cafés, well worth making a special effort to visit. This part of Pimlico still has a community atmosphere and sense of place that is a welcome change from the soulless office developments and heavy traffic of nearby Victoria.

Refreshment

If you're feeling peckish I strongly recommend a piece of pizza and a cappuccino at *Gastronomia Italia*, on Upper Tachbrook Street, which also has tables outside on fine days. *Bar Fresco*, just around the corner on Longmore Street, is also a very good café. If you fancy an alcoholic beverage, *The Page* is just opposite the market and is a modern style pub.

Local Attractions

Despite the subdued nature of the market, the area is still very much worth a visit if only to escape the polluted and crowded mayhem around Victoria Station. If you like hunting for second-hand bargains there are five excellent charity shops in the area: *FARA* and *Retromania* on Tachbrook Street, *Oxfam* on Warwick Way, *Trinity Hospice Shop* on Wilton Road and the wonderful *Crusade* which has moved to Churton Street following the redevelopment of Lower Tachbrook Street.

Getting a Stall

For further details contact Westminster Council (see appendix)

Whitecross Street

OLD STREET

Whitecross Street, between Old Street and Errol Street. EC1
Tube: Old Street (Northern); Barbican (Metropolitan and Circle)
Rail: Old Street
Open: Monday-Friday 10am-2.30pm

Whitecross Street is a place where several different worlds intermingle, with smart city workers coming here to shop and have lunch rubbing shoulders with the locals who live in the housing estates nearby. The market is not difficult to find: to the north is the recently renovated St Luke's Church and to the south loom the huge Barbican Towers. The lunch time market that runs between these landmarks once extended the entire length of Whitecross Street but has gradually declined to just a handful of stalls with the market only starting at the junction with Banner Street. It is here that the only fruit and veg stall is located, providing a good selection of everyday basics as well as one or two exotic ingredients such as pak choy and chicory. Peter has been working on the stall for over 30 years and has witnessed the market's gradual decline. When he started on the market there were many stalls fighting for the passing custom, but now his stall stands alone on this part of the street and things are a lot quieter. When asked to explain the

Whitecross Street

market's decline he is certain, "I blame the supermarkets, people prefer to buy things with a card these days".

Further south along Whitecross Street there are a mix of stalls offering household goods, CDs and DVDs, toys, smaller electrical items, tools and a stall offering cheap casual and smart clothing. One of the clothing stalls had reduced all garments to £10 and was awash with shoppers in search of a bargain. The stall flogging cheap books and mags is great value with lots of recently published mags for only 50p each, although sadly this stall is vulnerable to the weather and doesn't show up if it's grim. One of the best stalls sells all kinds of things from plastic crates spread along the pavement but is another trader that does not always show up at the market.

Part of the market is situated under the canopy of the shopping precinct on the corner of Errol Street just outside Waitrose. The pedestrian square is given over to a handful of large stalls offering bags, CDs, towels and bedding, underwear and a mixture of casual and smart clothing. Among the bargains to be found here were good quality baseball hats for £4, nylon rucksacks for £6 and smart ladies leather boots for only £20. One stall was selling a selection of new cookbooks by famous names like Hester Blumenthal and Jamie Oliver for just £10.

Whitecross Street appears to be a market in a state of terminal decline with the only sign of improvement being the burgeoning number of fast food stalls to cater for the nearby office workers looking for a cheap lunch. The area is in a state of flux at the moment with several new art galleries and some attempts to smarten up the street while other buildings lie empty and neglected. Islington Council is not indifferent to the markets plight and does promote regular food markets on Thursdays and Fridays which has provided a temporary injection of vitality into a market that has faced years of gradual decline.

Refreshment

As well as being home to a string of café's, chippies and take-aways, Whitecross Street boasts a few upmarket eateries: *Carnevale*, an award-winning vegetarian restaurant serving hot and cold food to eat in or take away; *Tassili* (on the right, just off the main road on Roscoe Street) serves up Mediterranean-style lunches and snacks; and *Pham Sushi* is a new sushi restaurant that is always busy at lunch time. *The Cosy* has been on the street for donkey's years and offers good quality traditional fish and chips. Alternatively, if the weather is fine, buy a take-away from one of the many food stalls and head back north to the grounds of *St Luke's* which is an excellent place enjoy an alfresco lunch.

Local Attractions

There are two major attractions in this part of town; the *Barbican Centre* which hosts all kinds of arts and entertainments behind its red brick façade and *The Museum of London* which is about ten minutes walk from the market. *St Luke's* has been renovated in recent years and is now the home to the *London Symphony Orchestra* which gives regular lunch time concerts.

Getting a Stall

For further details contact Islington Council (see appendix).

North

Alfie's Antiques Market

13-25 Church Street, NW8

Tube: Edgware Road / Marylebone (Bakerloo)
Open: Tuesday-Saturday 10am-6pm

Alfie's is situated in the midst of Church Street Market and acts as a fascinating contrast with its more down-to-earth neighbour. Within this lofty five storey Edwardian building can be found over 70 dealers selling jewellery, furniture, costume and retro clothing, lighting, tableware, objets d'art, paintings, clocks and books. Among the most interesting things found here on a recent visit were a set of two Italian, cherry wood armchairs re-upholstered in purple velvet and dating from the 1950's. The chairs were wonderful and had a price tag of £1750 which was reasonable given their quality and rarity. Two decent armchairs from Habitat would probably set you back a similar amount and would seem dull in comparison. Similarly the dealer specialising in lighting had a spectacular range of large steel angle-poise lamps for up to £195, which might seem expensive, but these lamps were design classics that looked as though they could last a lifetime.

If such things are a little beyond your budget there was solace to be found at a nearby concession where a very tidy little 1950's coffee table was only £35. Likewise, wandering through the labyrinthine maze and particularly on the upper storeys, I found plenty of traders dealing in attractive smaller items with lower price tags. Among these were several good costume jewellery dealers with lots of appealing goodies to sift through for £3-£4.

There is now just one book dealers at Alfie's offering anything from tatty old Penguin paperbacks to elegant leather-bound tombs. Several art dealers ply their trade here, but I was particularly drawn to the poster dealer with huge French advertising posters of the 1920's and 30's adorning his walls. A large poster was several hundred pounds, but Gallic style is an expensive commodity.

Alfie's certainly has a good deal of charm. The dealers are friendly, knowledgeable and occasionally eccentric, the building is huge with numerous staircases and various levels within each storey and there is even an iron staircase with glass roof and a small water feature on the ground floor. Another good thing about Alfie's is its diversity with lots of 20th century items as well as the more traditional antiques for which it is better known.

Refreshment

Alfie's has an excellent roof top café which does a selection of Mediterranean food as well as established British favourites and has seating both inside and out.

Local Attractions

The main attraction in this part of town is Church Street Market (see page 64).

Getting a Stall

For further details contact Alfie's office on 020 7723 6066.

Camden

a) The Stables Market
b) Camden Lock Market
c) Camden Market

Tube: Camden Town, Chalk Farm
Open: Various times, see each market for details, but Saturday is the biggest day

On the stretch of Camden High Street from Camden Town tube station to Harmood Street there are five separate markets but most people know them collectively as Camden Market. Camden is known throughout Europe as a place of hedonism, fashion and music and this reputation draws vast crowds of teenagers and young adults to the area every weekend. Visiting Camden at its busiest you can see every form of haircut from Punks sporting Mohicans to Goths with complicated creations involving hair extensions. Those with grey hair or a bald pate are a rarity here and the older people that you see are usually anxious parents accompanying their young on a shopping trip. Camden is now dedicated to all the things that youth find interesting with lots of fashion stalls, CD dealers, retro clothing, fashion footwear, jewellery and accessories, pot smoking paraphernalia, posters and lots of tourist souvenirs.

Camden is a place that is constantly changing and this is most evident at the northern end of the market where in recent years Camden Lock has a new glass roof on its formerly open courtyard and the Stables has been completely redeveloped and is still undergoing a major refurbishment which will see a new shopping complex built in the structure of the old railway arches. Regrettably not all the recent changes have been good ones and in February 2008 the Canal Market was burnt down – the site is now boarded-up and awaiting redevelopment.

Regardless of the fires and increased commercialisation of Camden and its markets there seems little that can stop the place from growing in popularity. The Camden scene can be bewildering to the older generation, but to the young it is one of London's major destinations.

Refreshment

Inverness Street has a number of trendy cafés where you can relax and get a drink. Each part of the market has a good choice of food stalls with the Stables and Camden Lock Market having a particularly wide choice with food from around the World. All the big chains have a piece of the pie here from *Belgo* to *Pizza Express* to *Wagamama*. *Dingwalls/Bar* in Middle Yard at Camden Lock Market is a great place for a fair-weather pint. *Yum Chaa* is located on the first floor of Camden Lock courtyard and is a great place to go for tea and cake. For a post-shopping escape, head to *Marine Ices* at 8 Haverstock Hill near Chalk Farm tube. Not just a purveyor of fine ice creams, but also of cheap and tasty Italian pastas, pizzas and salads.

Local Attractions

The canal that runs through Camden extends from Little Venice in the west to Islington in the north. It can be picked up at Camden Lock and is a great way to escape the crowds. For a pleasant, relaxed trip down the waterway, hop on a canal boat at the Camden Lock stop. The boat route extends between London Zoo in Regent's Park and Little Venice. Try *Regent's Canal Waterbus* (tel. 020 7482 2550), *Jason's Trips* (tel. 020 7286 3428), or *Jenny Wren's Canal Boat Cruises* (tel. 020 7485 4433).

Stables Market

Camden Lock

Camden Market

Stables Market

Stables Market

The Electric Ballroom

184 Camden High Street
www.electricballroom.co.uk
Open: Saturday-Sunday 9am-5pm

The Electric Ballroom is a nightclub and music venue which opens its doors to the public at the weekends as part of Camden market. The Ballroom is not as commercial as some parts of the market and has become a refuge for the cheaper second-hand clothing stalls that cannot afford the high rents charged elsewhere. This makes the it a great place to look for clothing bargains with one stall recently offering lots of garments for just £15 and even reducing some items to £5. As well as retro clothing there are also several traders selling designer jewellery, new street fashion and a music stall playing club anthems to attract interest. The Goth fashion stall is always busy with pale youngsters trying out the latest addition to their wardrobe. The Ballroom deserves to be better known and is certainly one of the most interesting parts of Camden Market at the weekend. On occasional weekends the venue is given over to other events such as record fairs, so check the website before making a special trip.

Getting a Stall

For more details contact the market office on 020 7485 9006

Camden Market

Camden High Street, south of Buck Street
Open: Thursday-Sunday 9am-5.30pm

This small square containing about one hundred stalls is the first outdoor market the crowds encounter after disgorging from Camden tube. The place is always packed at the weekends with teenagers from all over the world. There are a few good stalls here selling original clothing, but they are difficult to find among the comic T-shirts, cheap sunglasses and pot smoking paraphernalia. I liked the hand-made skirts for about £30 and the designer making her own Goth inspired garments for considerably more. There were also a few music stalls playing their wares and contributing to fashionable vibe. Teenagers love this place, but those with a mortgage and responsibilities will be appalled. If you don't like crowds, you should visit on Thursday or Friday when it's a lot quieter.

Getting a Stall

Phone the market office on 020 7267 3417 for details.

THE ELECTRIC MARKET

ABOUT US

The Electric Market has been open in the heart of Camden Town for 25 years now, which makes it pretty well established.

Being an indoor market it's ideal for shopping in our famously unreliable British weather. The market is easy to find – just moments away from Camden Town tube station. A great first stop on a shopping trip to Camden.

www.electricballroom.co.uk

184 Camden High St, NW1
Open: Sat-Sun 9am-5pm
Nearest tube: Camden Town

WHAT'S ON

There are over 50 stalls inside, selling an eclectic mix of:

fashion, unique pieces by independent designers, club wear, retro clothing, jewellery, T-Shirts, accessories, leather, badges, fake furs, CD's, records & posters

WHERE

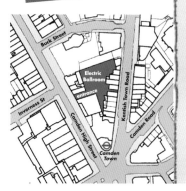

Inverness Street Market
See entry on page 72.

Camden Canal Market
Northeast of the canal, and south of Castle Haven Road
This part of the market suffered a fire in February 2008 and is currently a charred ruin awaiting redevelopment.

Camden Lock Market
Northwest of Camden Lock
www.camdenlockmarket.com
Open: Tuesday-Sunday 10am-6pm, Thursday till 7pm.
This is where Camden Market started as a few humble stalls in 1975. In the years that have followed the market has grown and developed into a complex maze of yards containing shops and stalls offering a mixture of arts and crafts, new clothing, jewellery, vinyl and an assortment of novelty gifts. Things are a lot more professional these days with traders displaying their wares with some care and few of the disorganised second-hand stalls that were once a feature of the market.

It is easy to loose your way in Camden Lock which is made up of a smart *Market Hall* with two floors of shops encircles by three interconnected squares called *East Yard*, *Middle Yard* and *West Yard*. The *East Yard* has recently acquired a stylish glass roof to keep out the rain which is another indication that this place becoming smarter. The market ends with an avenue of stalls in *Camden Lock Place* marking the start of the Stables Market with its new glass fronted office building.

The yard furthest away from the High Street is called the *West Yard* and can be accessed by a narrow footbridge which runs across the canal behind Starbucks. This courtyard has a number of interesting permanent units including *Black Gull* second-hand bookshop and the retro accessories store *Berty & Gertie*. The stalls here are also worth inspection with some good jewellery to be found including a range of contemporary silver items from *Sakamoto Designs* for as little as £6.50 for a pair of ear rings. There are also stalls selling stylish street fashion, hats, pottery and a lone retro stall offering cowboy boots for only £10. The rest of the yard (about two thirds) is dedicated to food with cuisine from around the world and several permanent cafés including the wonderful *Yum Chaa* for traditional tea and cake.

The *Middle Yard* is more of a thoroughfare with just a handful of stalls offering new street fashion and one lone second-hand stall selling books, CD's and bric-à-brac with the proceeds going to charity. The

Market Hall is the large Victorian factory that has been converted into part of the market and is accessed via steps from the *Middle Yard*. The building contains about 70 stalls on two levels with the emphasis upon arts and crafts. Here you can find colourful hand-painted silk ties, contemporary oil paintings of London life, scented candles, leather bound note pads, hand-made jewellery and a variety of contemporary bags.

The *West Yard* is a small but compact square of about 40 stalls offering a continuation of the arts and crafts to be found in the *Market Hall* which surrounds it. Among the stalls are good quality jewellery, street fashion, posters and the occasional bargain such as the contemporary cushions in bright colours which were reduced to only £2 each and the quality hemp T-shirts which were only £3 each. The vinyl stall not only offered reasonably priced music but also provided a musical backdrop to the shopping.

By cutting back through the Market Hall you get to *Camden Lock Place* which is the dividing line between Camden Lock and the vast glass structure that marks the beginning of The Stables Market. This cobbled avenue has a good selection of stalls largely dealing in fashion and ethnic gear. Recently one of the stalls was offering Converse boots from only £25 while another had multi-coloured Indian sofa throws for a reasonable £20. The doughnut and fruit juice stalls at the High Street end of the avenue are a permanent and popular feature and can be found just below the bridge which proclaims CAMDEN LOCK in bright orange letters.

Getting a Stall

Camden Lock Market Office
56 Camden Lock Place, West Yard, NW1 8AF
Tel: 020 7284 2084
You can turn up at the market at 9.45am on a weekday or 9am on a weekend and usually get a stall, but it's a good idea to ring the market office first.

The Stables Market

West of Chalk Farm Road and opposite Hartland Road
Open: Daily 9am-5pm, busiest at weekends

The Stables Market has been transformed in recent years and is currently undergoing further building work to create a large, modern shopping piazza with an internet café, music store and several large retro clothing outlets. This is the second stage of a process that began with the transformation of the area between Camden Lock and the railway arches where a glass fronted office complex now rises above a maze of shopping avenues lined with permanent units offering fashion, music, jewellery and accessories, interspersed with numerous fast food outlets. Following the passageways that lead into the old Stables the second-hand clothes and bric-à-brac have disappeared and the place has been transformed into something closer to an alternative shopping centre rather than a market. The hordes of teenagers that pack the stables every weekend enjoy looking for new clothing, alternative music, jewellery and accessories without any concern for what has disappeared. Amid all the African carvings, papier-mâché piggie banks and ethnic clothing and household goods there was one interesting second-hand outlet called *Curiosity* which had a good selection of clothing, books and bric-à-brac to sift through.

Getting a stall
Stables Market Office, Stables Market Ltd, 27 Stanley Sidings, Chalk Farm Road, NW1 8AH   Tel: 020 7485 5511

THE STABLES MARKET

over 450 shops
50 food shops

0207 485 5511
Open 7 days a week
Nearest Tube:
Chalk Farm Road
Camden High Street
(north of the Railway Bridge)

Stables Camden Market remains London's second largest tourist attraction with over 35 million foot flow per annum.

Camden Passage

Opposite Islington Green at the junction of Upper Street and Essex Road, Islington, N1

Tube: Angel (Northern)
Open: Wednesday and Saturday 7am-3pm (antique market); Thursday 8.30am-6pm (book market)

Camden Passage is not anywhere near Camden, but lies in a quaint pedestrian passage that runs behind Islington High Street. The modest shop fronts, largely occupied by antique dealers, and the flagstone paving give an old world atmosphere and the antique market on Wednesday and Saturday and the book market on Thursday add to this sense of antiquity. The architecture is genuine Victorian and Edwardian, but the market and antique dealers are far more recent, arriving in the 1960s – when Islington began the process of gentrification that has transformed it into one of London's most desirable neighbourhoods.

The twice weekly antique market is still going but has been diminished by recent developments at the Essex Road end of the passage. It was here that a small square with glass roof provided shelter for the market when at its largest on Saturdays and also acted as the venue for a Sunday Farmers' Market. The roof has been removed and the square is now a less welcoming place with stalls setting up on a Saturday against the wishes of the smart new boutiques that have moved here and the farmers' market has upped sticks and found a site in the playground of a nearby school (see page 227).

Despite these problems the antiques market is still a lot of fun to visit with experienced antique dealers selling genuine antiques and objets d'art along side itinerant traders offering junk on the pavement for just a few pounds. The mix is an appealing one with lots of junk to sift through for the occasional gem as well as some exquisite items sold at a much higher price. Prices can range from a several hundred pounds for a fine Art Deco lamp to just £3 for an old wood carving picked up at a stall offering piles of bric-à-brac with very little effort made to display the ramshackle stock. Those with more money to spend and an interest in fine antiques should concentrate on the far ends of the market. At the southern end stands Pierrepont Arcade – a covered area with al fresco stalls and an indoor maze of units selling little bits and pieces like stamps and military medals. It is in the middle section of the market just before the Camden Head pub that the more junky stalls tend to congregate with enough second-hand clothes, junk and bric-à-brac to keep bargain hunters occupied for while.

On the way along Camden Passage, you'll find a lovely collection of little shops selling prints, furniture and antique dresses. *Annie's Vintage Clothes* and *Cloud Cuckoo Land* at the junction with Charlton Place both sell dreamy vintage dresses and accessories. *Annie's* has a bent towards Victorian era and early 19th-century clothing while *Cloud Cuckoo Land* sells wonderfully exuberant 1940s, '50s and '60s garb. The street also houses a few shops selling sumptuous art nouveau and art deco jewellery as well stallholders who hawk similar decorative items.

The book market on Thursdays has a completely different feel. While the antique market sells mostly upmarket items to tourists and well-to-do antique hunters, the book market is far more egalitarian. Hardbacks sell for £4 and paperbacks go for a £1 or less. Don't expect decorative antiquarian tomes, but rather popular titles from well-known writers as well as books on travel, art, cooking and history.

Camden Passage

Refreshment

A stop at the *Camden Head* pub with its original Victorian swirly etched glass windows and burgundy velvet banquette seating is the perfect end to a market trip. There's a small terrace with picnic benches for warm weather drinking. The only unfortunate feature to this otherwise stunning pub is the flashing game machines in the corner. For more sustenance, simply step out to Upper Street running parallel to Camden Passage to find a plethora of restaurants and cafés serving everything from Thai to French food.

Getting a Stall

For a stand at the antiques market phone 020 7359 0190.

Chalton Street

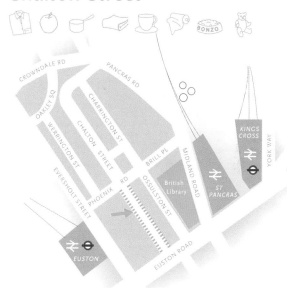

North • Chalton Street

Chalton Street, between Euston Road and Churchway, NW1
Tube: Euston (Northern, Victoria), King's Cross (Piccadilly, Metropolitan, Circle, Northern)
Open: Friday 12noon-2pm

Located just off the busy Euston Road, Chalton Street and its Friday market are easily missed. Despite the prestige of the nearby British Library, this area – known as Somers Town – is a poor and rather run-down part of London. The majority of shops are boarded up or empty, making the Friday market a much anticipated event for the local Indian and Pakistani communities who live on the surrounding estates and who, along with the local office workers, comprise the majority of this market's custom.

The market used to run throughout the week, but cutting trading down to a Friday lunchtime has condensed a week's slow activity into a hectic shopping experience packed into a few short hours. Among the twenty or so stalls, there's a lot to catch the eye including basic fashion clothing, shoes, fabrics by the metre, pet food and toys, exotic fruit and veg with plenty of fresh herbs, good value kitchenware and a stall specialising in household cleaning materials and toiletries at a fraction of High Street prices. The large beach towels sold at the towel and bedding stall for just £6 were a good deal as were the women's bags sold in large piles from a couple of tables for just £2 each. There are several good fabric stalls with one at the far end of the market (away from Euston Road) always busy with local Asian women sifting through the reams – many of which are priced at £1 per metre. The shoe stall is a regular attraction and offers a good selection of ladies footwear for a fiver a pair.

Chalton Street is strong on basic street clothing, but most of the stuff on offer is of the cheap and cheerful variety aimed at the limited pockets of the neighbourhood. For example, most T-shirts are about £2 each and it's very difficult to find one for over a fiver. Value and low price being the name of the game, the old man at the end of the market was doing a roaring trade in an assortment of disparate things from jumbo packs of toilet roll for just £1 to attractive, large enamel flower pots for the same price.

Chalton Street is still an interesting market to visit on a Friday lunchtime. Although most of the retail shops have closed, there are lots of cafés catering for the office workers of the area on their lunch breaks, making the market a good place to shop and then relax afterwards with a good cappuccino or something to eat.

Refreshment

Café Bella is a fancy establishment at the Euston Road end of the market, but next-door is the more basic and good value *King's Café*. Just opposite these two is a very nice Italian café called *Albertini* and further along is the more traditional *Pinner Café*. At the far end of the market is a new pub called, rather confusingly, *The Somers Town Coffee House*.

Local Attractions

The only major attraction in this part of town is the wonderful British Library which is just a few minutes walk east along Euston Road.

Getting a Stall

For further details contact Camden Council (see appendix).

Chapel Market

Between Liverpool Road and Penton Street, N1

Tube: Angel (Northern)

Open: Tuesday to Saturday 9am-6pm; Thursday and Sunday 9am-4pm

This street has hosted a vibrant local market since around 1870 and despite the many changes that have transformed Islington – particularly in the last 40 years – the market is still going strong. At the Liverpool Road end there is a Sainsbury's and Marks & Spencer as well as the Angel Shopping Centre, but the competition seems to be good for the street. Chapel is one of the few markets busy during the week with around 60 stalls offering an interesting mix of food, clothing, bedding, books, shoes and accessories.

The fruit and veg stalls are still a big draw for the locals with many of the traders making an effort to display their stock and offering a range of produce that any supermarket would struggle to match. Many of the traders also offer a bit of banter free of charge with several still calling out their wears – 'come on ladies avacodo 60p a pop, nice n' ripe. Come n taste me ripe avos' – which is something you won't hear in the fruit and veg isle of your local supermarket. Chapel is one of the few markets that also provide a much wider range of food with several fish mongers, a specialist French cheese stall and two deli stalls offering a good choice of salamis, olives and other delicious treats at very competitive prices.

Chapel Market also has a reasonable selection of fashion stalls offering the usual mix of good value street fashion, bags, shoes and accessories. There are usually a few fashion bargains to be found with colourful T-shirts for just £2 and a good choice of seasonal footwear for under a tenner, but the emphasis is definitely towards the young and fashion conscious. The haberdashers is always good value with lots of ribbons and lace for just 50p a metre and a good selection of buttons to sift through. Chapel has its fair share of stalls offering cheap bedding, but unlike most markets it also has a stall selling whole beds with five examples placed on the street for punters to try and free delivery included in the price. If your interested in bedding of a different kind, the market has an excellent plant stall with lots of healthy looking plants for just a few quid and plenty of free advice if you need it.

In Chapel Market's heyday the stalls would extend the entire length of the street and onto the side streets but now things are a little quieter and the market tends to peter out at Baron Street. It is here that the market's sole second-hand book dealer offers a mix of fact and fiction for a reasonable but not cheap price. It is a pity to see the far end of the street so quiet, but there is always enough activity at the Liverpool Road end to make this one of London's best local markets.

Refreshment

There are several good take-away stalls on the market with the baked potato stall being a long established favourite. If you want to sit down *Euphorium Bakery* is excellent for pastries, sandwiches and coffee while the *Daisy Café* on White Conduit Street is a great local caff. Off the beaten path but nearby on Penton Street is the outstanding *Olga Stores*, a cramped Italian deli selling scrumptious Italian meats, cheeses and dry goods. *The Agricultural* at the junction with Liverpool Road is fine for a pint.

Local Attractions

If you like unusual shopping experiences don't miss the junk shop on White Conduit Street which has all kinds of oddities, books and clothing behind its cluttered windows. *The Candid Arts Trust* at 3 Torrens Street – just behind Angel tube – hosts regular exhibitions and has a very good café.

Getting a Stall

For further details contact Islington Council (see appendix).

Chapel Market

Church Street

Church Street from Edgware Road to Lisson Grove, NW8 &W2
Tube: Edgware Road (District, Metropolitan and Bakerloo)
Open: Tuesday-Saturday 9am-5pm

Church Street Market occupies a fairly central location, but few people outside the immediate area actually visit it and if they do it is usually by accident on the way to the more famous Alfie's Antique Market which lies at the Lisson Grove end of the street. For this reason, Church Street Market has managed to maintain a friendly community feel, with lots of the stall-holders taking time out to have a natter with regular customers on quiet weekdays. On Saturdays the market greatly increases in size with stalls extending the entire length of Church Street and the crowds making it a very exciting experience, but offering traders little time for a leisurely chat.

This part of the Edgware Road (just past the Marylebone fly-over) is pretty down at heel and many of the stalls concentrate on the cheap and cheerful rather than better quality goods. There are lots of good deals to be found with the £5 shoe stall at the Edgware Road entrance to the market always popular. Church Street is a good market to stock up on basic fresh fruit and veg, but there is not much of the exotic on offer. There is more choice when it comes to fish with three stalls setting up here on a Saturday offering anything from the humble cod

Church Street

to juicy king prawns and fresh squid. Further along at the junction with Penfold Street there is a young man selling farm fresh eggs, jars of honey and fruit cake from a traditional wooden stall that was handed on to him from his mother who was a character at the market for many years. One trader sells surplus and slightly damaged biscuits, chocolates and other packaged foods. The service is gruff and sometimes abusive, but with lots of bargains he is always busy.

Although many of the clothes on offer on Church Street are cheap and tacky, there are several stalls selling interesting stuff. One displayed a wide range of designer T-shirts (probably copies) for only a tenner and another was offering M&S suits for just £50. Other items for sale include pet food and toys, household goods, children's clothes, fresh flowers, underwear, bedding and towels and several good value bag stalls stocking anything from rucksacks to suitcases.

At the junction with Salisbury Street, Church Street undergoes a subtle transformation as modern buildings give way to well preserved 19th century shop fronts, many of them dealing in fine antiques. It is at this part of the market that you'll find Alfie's Antiques Market with five floors of antiques and a roof-top café (see page 44). The fly traders that once sold jewellery and bric-à-brac outside Alfie's have long ago been driven from the street by the actions of Westminster Council. It is a pity as this part of the market could do with a few second-hand stalls to add a bit of variety. The best thing about this part of the market is the excellent fabric stall selling basic material for as little as 50p a metre and there are one or two good fashion stalls on a Saturday offering fashionable seasonal ladies wear with colourful summer dresses recently drawing a large crowd for just a tenner.

Church Street market is one of the most interesting and vibrant local markets in London and certainly deserves to be more widely known. The market builds momentum from towards the end of the week with Saturday the best day to visit if you want to see the place at its best.

Refreshment

Church Street has no smart restaurants but is awash with simple, good value eating places. *The Market Grill*, which serves both English and Thai food, is a popular place on market days with a surprising number of burly market traders preferring a bowl of Thai noodles to a traditional fry-up. For a coffee in a more stylish environment try *Cali Café*, near *Alfie's Antiques Market*. *Alfie's* also has a very pleasant roof-top café which does great food and has seating both inside and out. The market also has several fast food stalls offering cuisine from around the world. *The Traders Inn* is a popular traditional boozer if you fancy a pint.

Local Attractions

Alfie's Antiques Market is also well worth a visit with its fabulous collection of clothes, pictures, jewellery, furniture and books (see page 44 for further details).

Getting a Stall

For further details contact Westminster City Council (see appendix).

Hampstead Community Market

Hampstead Community Centre, 78 Hampstead High Street, NW3
Tube: Hampstead (Northern)
Open: Saturday 10am-6pm (food market), Sunday 10am-6pm, (first of month – antiques; second of month – books; third and fourth of month – arts and crafts)

This market acquired a reputation for offering cheap tea, coffee and a comforting selection of homemade cakes - all served with brisk efficiency by a team of old ladies. The centre was a great place to escape the homogenised, over-priced coffee bars of Hampstead, but the collectables market was a rather subdued affair with about eight stalls showing up at the weekend.

The market management have decided to take the bull by the horns and make some fundamental changes to boost the market's appeal. On Saturdays there is now a food market offering meat, cheese, olives and preserves – complimenting the long established food stalls on the High Street which sell fresh fruit and veg, fish and take-away food. The Sunday market continues to offer arts, crafts and collectables on the last two weekends of each month, but there is now a changing itinerary with antiques on the first Sunday and a specialist book market on the second Sunday of each month.

The market was certainly in need of a re-vamp and hopefully this new series of specialist markets can give the Community Centre the injection of vitality it has been lacking in the last few years.

Hampstead Community Market

Local Attractions

Exclusivo is a second-hand designer clothes shop on Flask Walk. Ignore the dreadful Euro-tat name and head on in for a good rummage. There is also a good *Oxfam* shop on Gayton Road which is worth a visit for designer cast-offs. For more antiques and collectables the *Hampstead Antique and Craft Emporium* is just around on Heath Street.

Getting a Stall

For further details contact the Community Centre on 020 7794 8313 or e-mail hcc.camden@virgin.net.

Hoxton Street

Hoxton Street, between Falkirk Street and Nuttall Street, N1
Tube: Old Street (Northern)
Rail: Old Street
Open: Monday-Saturday 9am-4pm (main day Saturday)

Hoxton has a reputation for being ultra-trendy, but the fashion, and money that goes with it, does not extend further north than Hoxton Square. The contrast is most apparent on a busy Saturday when you can walk along Hoxton Street through the busy market full of locals from the surrounding estates doing their shopping and then carry on into Hoxton Square where trendies, models and photographers can be found discussing their latest "project" over a cappuccino. Although the two worlds are just a few minutes walk from each other there is little sign that they mix. It's a pity that the fashionable people that hang out on Hoxton Square and no doubt espouse working-class solidarity, are not to be seen shopping at one of London's traditional street markets.

During the week it would be hard to tell that a market trades on Hoxton Street with just a handful of stalls showing up. It is really on a Saturday that the market takes over, with the street turned into a pedestrian area from the corner of Shenfield Street to the juction with Nuttall Street. On a Saturday the market has a real atmosphere with crowds milling between the various stalls featuring a decent selection of street fashion, fruit and veg, flowers, bedding and towels, underwear, shoes, bags, CDs and DVDs and a solitary fresh fish stall.

The market does not have a spectacular range of clothing, but among the unexceptional stalls some good deals and some reasonable quality goods can be found. One trader was busy selling all kinds of underware from cardboard boxes with three pairs of sock for £1 and all knickers for the same price. Piles of end-of-season street fashion were eagerly sifted through by a small crowd in search of bargains with quite a few emerging from the scrum with an armful of clothes for less than a tenner. There are quite a few stalls selling good quality high street fashion all sold for a fraction of the original price. A rail of Top Shop raincoats was originally reduced to £15 but had been knocked down to just £8, while another trader was offering Warehouse ladies slacks in lots of sizes for just £10 reduced from £40. Amid all the street fashion there are a number of genuinely quirky stalls with one old couple selling ex-display designer frames for just £20 a pair and another offering an assortment of second-hand shoes for just £5 a pair.

The rest of the market caters for the everyday needs of the local population with the emphasis on low prices rather than quality or diversity. The fruit and veg is fresh but basic, the CDs and DVDs are reasonably priced but only very mainstream stuff, and the duvet covers and towels are mostly in garish colours and synthetic fibres. Likewise the cosmetics are all very cheap and sold quite brazenly as copies with perfumes going for only £4 a bottle. The household goods stalls are all dirt cheap and you can't go wrong with large rolls of dustbin bags for just £1 and two face clothes for the same price.

Hoxton is still a good local market on a Saturday, but it has not been immune from the changes in shopping that have hit all local markets in recent years. The stalls now peters out before Falkirk Street and the quirky second-hand stalls that were once a feature here have long disappeared. There have been a few improvements such as the erection of grand iron gates proclaiming the market and the opening of several smart cafés on the street. Walking south the skyline dramatically changes as the vast buildings known as 'the cheese grater' and 'gherkin' come into view. A reminder that this little market is not far from the wealth and prestige of the City.

Hoxton Market

Refreshment

For something to eat, try either *F. Cooke* for pie and mash, *Red House* for a good cappuccino or one of the market's many greasy spoons - the most popular being *Paula's Café*. The West Indian stall on the junction with Shenfield Street is a long standing feature of the market offering delicious barbecue food.

Local Attractions

Hoxton Market no longer trades in second-hand goods, but if you are looking for interesting junk visit Kingsland Waste (see page 194) which is ten minutes walk along Kingsland Road. Hoxton Square is an attractive place to relax with lots of bars and several fashionable art galleries including *White Cube* at number 48.

Getting a Stall

For further details contact Hackney Council (see appendix).

Inverness Street

Between Camden High Street and Arlington Road, NW1

Tube: Camden Town (Northern Line)
Open: Monday-Saturday 8.30am-5pm

Inverness Street used to be a relatively quiet local market selling good quality food amid the fashion markets of Camden (see page 72). The market has been going since 1900 but these days the popularity of Camden as a centre for music and fashion has subsumed Inverness Street and most of the stalls now sell the same kind of street fashion that can be found in other Camden Markets. A couple of the better quality fruit and veg stalls are still going strong but they are now surrounded by take-away food and fashion stalls.

The change has given the market a new lease of life and although it is a pity to loose some of Camden's diversity it is good to see the street packed on a Saturday with people enjoying the shopping. The stall specialising in colourful ladies street fashion was doing good business with most dresses for around a tenner and several discount rails with garments reduced to only £2.99 or two for a fiver. There were several stalls competing for the lucrative T-shirts market and in a moment of weakness I paid £12 for a T-shirt proclaiming 'the Dude abides'. Those more interested in football than the films of the Coen brothers may find what their heart desires at the football memorabilia stall which is a long established feature of the market and always a centre of attention on match days.

Inverness Street

Refreshment

There are now several take-away stalls on the market offering Italian pasta, French crépes or Mexican tacos for reasonable prices. If you fancy a sit down there are lots of trendy cafés on Inverness Street among them *Made in Brazil* which serves a good cappuccino. For something a little stronger *The Good Mixer* at the far end of the street is a popular drinking hole.

Getting a Stall

For further details contact Camden Council (see appendix).

Kilburn Square

**Kilburn High Road between
Brondesbury Road
& Victoria Road, NW6**

Tube: Kilburn Park (Bakerloo)
Rail: Kilburn High Road
Open: Monday-Saturday 9am-5.30pm

Kilburn Market was a fairly ugly 1980s construction situated next to the busy Kilburn High Road. The place was always friendly but the series of lock-up units offered a pretty average range of cheap goods, supplementing the functional selection on offer on the busy High Street. Here you could find the usual mix of fruit and veg, new clothes, plants and flowers, household goods and toiletries, bedding and towels, jewellery, hair accessories, hats, carpets, luggage and electrical goods.

At the time of going to press the market was due to be redeveloped. Flats are to be built above the old market and a new courtyard created with a continuation of the units at ground level. The market is still running at present, but all the traders are preparing for closure. It is hoped that the new development will provide a brighter and more pleasant environment for the market to re-establish itself in the years to come.

Getting a Stall

The market is privately run by Hazeldean Properties, for more details about the current state of the development and the possibility of future trading contact the market manager on 01753 663 313 or 07768 206 754.

Nag's Head

South side of Seven Sisters Road at Holloway Road junction, N7
Tube: Holloway Road (Piccadilly)
Open: Monday, Tuesday, Thursday 9am-5pm (new and second-hand goods market); Wednesday 9am-3.30pm (second-hand and antiques market); Friday-Saturday 9am-5pm (new goods market), Sunday 7am-2pm (flea market)

Nestled behind the Nag's Head shopping centre with its main entrance on bustling Seven Sisters Road, this market has been fighting competition from the surrounding shops for years. Nag's Head Market might seem like an afterthought to the main shopping complex, but it began trading on the site in the mid 70s before the shopping centre was built and looks destined to outlast its neighbours, which are due for redevelopment. The market has survived by opening daily throughout the week and offering different themes depending on the day with the flea markets proving very popular on Wednesdays and Sundays.

The emphasis of the market may change from day to day, but there are lots of regular stalls that trade every day selling necessities such as food, household goods, and new clothing. The excellent fruit and veg outlet, fishmongers fabric stall and halal butchers are all popular features of the market. These permanent units are complimented by other stalls such as the egg man who has been selling farm fresh eggs here every Friday and Saturday for nearly 30 years. The cheap clothing stalls are suffering with competition from stores such as *Primark*, but Ali 'the sock man' keeps a smile on his face and hopes business will improve.

Wednesday is the biggest day, but its official status as an antiques market is a slight misnomer. It's certainly more of a second-hand market with stall upon stall selling used clothing. Women are well catered for with racks of dresses and labels varying from designer to High Street brands as well as a few vintage party dresses. There are also several stalls selling old records, vintage plates, and household accessories.

Nags Head Market is struggling on despite the competition and still seems to draw in the regulars with its unusual mix of new and second-hand shopping. There are plans to redevelop the shopping centre in the next few years, but the market is destined to keep on trading regardless of the upheaval going on around it.

Refreshment

The market has increased the number of stalls in recent years and now offers food from around the world with Brazilian, Italian and Caribbean stalls complimenting the traditional English caff. Away from the market on Holloway Road are the two *Amici* Italian cafés which are the best in the area.

Local Attractions

Bargain hunters visiting the market might also want to check out Rolls and Rems fabric shop (21 Seven Sisters Road). Further down the road away from Holloway Road is the Clarks Factory Shop (67-83 Seven Sisters Road) where bargain shoes for the whole family can be found.

Getting a Stall

Call the market manager on telephone 020 7607 3527 or stop by his office at the rear of the market.

Fresh Mackerel
£1.79 lb
£4.40 kg

Fresh
Bream
2 for £5
4 for £10

fresh Bass
2 for £5

Queen's Crescent

Queen's Crescent, between Malden Road and Grafton Road, NW5

Tube: Kentish Town or Chalk Farm (Northern Line)
Rail: Kentish Town West
Open: Thursday 8.30am-2.30pm and
Saturday (busiest day) 8.30am-3pm

Queen's Crescent is an anonymous street off the beaten track and easily missed. For this reason the market that takes place here on a Thursday and Saturday is a very local affair with people swapping gossip and news as they wander from stall to stall. The community is a mixture of Irish, Jamaican and Asian people, but the atmosphere is friendly and there is none of the tension witnessed at some of the larger markets.

Rival fruit and veg stalls mean some healthy bargains, and stockpiled bras, socks and undies all go for around a pound. Although unexciting, the other stalls are worth a look for good deals on new clothes, trainers, meat, flowers, bed linen, groceries, kitchen equipment, jewellery and even stationery. The stall selling bedding plants and cut flowers was good value with healthy looking rose bushes for just £2 and lots of small shrubs and plants for £1 each. At the Malden Road end of the market is a popular stall selling women's street fashion for just £5 a garment. Richard has been at the market on and off for over 18 years and has seen it gradually decline, 'people don't visit their local market in the way they used to – they used to call me Richie Rich now I'm Richie Poor…' and with a broad grin he was off to serve another customer.

Queen's Crescent is not the sort of market you would go to for anything particularly original and many of the stalls also trade from other markets during the week, but the local community atmosphere makes it a pleasant place to stroll and shop for basic essentials.

Refreshment

There are a few places to eat along the Crescent among them the *Blue Sea Fish Shop* and the *Gossip Stop Café* which is a busy greasy spoon caff. If you fancy something a little more spicy there is usually an Indian take-away stall on the market and for a drink *The Robert Peel* is probably your best bet.

Local Attractions

The Kentish Town City Farm is nearby in Cressfield Close for a temporary escape from city streets and Camden Market (see page 46) is a short bus ride away.

Getting a Stall

For further details contact Camden Council (see appendix).

Swiss Cottage

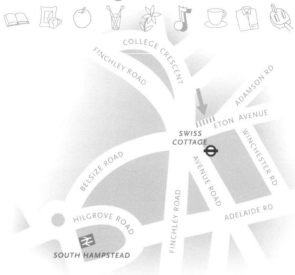

Eton Avenue (outside Hampstead Theatre), NW3
Tube: Swiss Cottage (Jubilee)
Rail: South Hampstead
Open: Friday & Saturday (busiest day) 9.30am-4.30pm, Wednesday
(farmers' market) 10am-4pm

Swiss Cottage market started in 1974 on undeveloped wasteland to the north of Swiss Cottage swimming pool and library and without the permission of Camden Council. The market was always run on a non-profit basis by an organisation set-up by the local community. It had a friendly and rather disorganised atmosphere with lots of interesting bookstalls, second-hand clothing and bric-à-brac to sift through among the 50 or so stalls. I remember visiting the market when I moved to London in the early 90s and being struck by this little oasis of 1970s hippy values amid the traffic of north London. The Market was always under threat from further office and property development and has relocated several times as the cranes have moved in and new buildings have gone up. In the last edition of this book the market was soldiering on despite being surrounded by building works for a new sports centre and flats.

The flats and sports complex are now finished but the new landscape has left no space for a market and the ten remaining stalls have been forced onto the pedestrian walkway outside Hampstead Theatre. The market is now run by Camden Council which limits trading to Friday and Saturday and has stopped all the second-hand dealers from trading. Despite these restrictions there are still a few interesting stalls. One of the most popular traders sells new designer labels at about half the original price with lots of bargains for those with enough money to profit from a Prada bag for £330, instead of £595, or a Gucci belt for £100, reduced from £190. The stall appears to have a loyal clientele among the wealthy fashion bargain hunters of Swiss Cottage. The second-hand book dealer is well worth visiting for a good selection of quality paperback fiction and a more limited range of factual and academic books. These two regular traders are joined by a reasonably priced jewellery stall, a trader selling cheap cosmetics, an organic fruit and veg stall and one specialising in New Age paraphernalia such as crystals and joss sticks. The other stalls are all concerned with food with *Flour Power* selling fresh breads and pastries and several other delicatessen stalls including a French couple that sell a delicious range of French produce such as eggs and bread.

It's a real pity to see what has happened to Swiss Cottage Market. The council went to some effort to accommodate the market on its new site and for a while the market got a new lease of life, but there has been a steady decline in the last few years. There may be some improvement with the arrival of a Farmer's Market on Wednesdays (see page 227) and there are plans for occasional French markets. The traders that do turn up here regularly, tell me that business has improved, so there is clearly some potential for the future.

Refreshment

The Thai food stall is one of the market's major attractions. If the weather is bad you could try the café in the *Hampstead Theatre*.

Local Attractions

The Freud Museum (20 Maresfield Gardens, tel: 020 7433 2002) is based at Freud's last home. The library across the square from the market is well worth a look at for its period piece interior. Sporty types might be attracted by the swimming pool and new gym.

Getting a Stall

For further details contact Camden Council (see appendix).

Wembley Sunday Market

Wembley Sunday Market

Stadium Car Park, Engineers Way, HA9

Website: www.wendyfairmarkets.com / www.wembleymarket.co.uk
Tube: Wembley Park (Metropolitan / Jubilee)
Open: Sunday 9am-4pm

As a child, my father used to take me to Wembley Stadium Market on a Sunday and buy me things like pens that write in three different colours or cheap plastic *Thunderbird* toys. I was always excited about going to the market and disappointed when the toy I had been campaigning for fell apart on the same afternoon. Since those halcyon days Wembley's twin towers have been reduced to rubble and a spectacular new stadium of steel and glass has emerged in its place. The market continues to trade in the car park outside the stadium and has kept its down-at-heel, fairground atmosphere with juddering generators, lively stallholders, the smell of doughnuts and burgers, and the pulse of musical from the CD stalls. It's still an exciting place to wander with the throng, but as with many Sunday car park markets (see Wimbledon Stadium page 127, and Nine Elms page 120) the experience lacks any charm and the goods are all new and mostly aimed at the budget shopper.

The one thing Wembley Market does have is choice, with lots of stalls competing – if one jacket isn't exactly what you want, there are many more stalls offering an alternative. Clothes in general are better

83

than average, with traders dealing in good value seconds like M&S dresses for £5 and M&S tops for £3. Many stalls offer teenage street fashion at low-commitment prices with a good choice of jeans, tops and several stalls offering brand name trainers from just £35. Wembley is also a good place to find cheap kid's clothes with deals such as track bottoms for £3.99 and tops for just £2.99

As befits any down-to-earth market, utility goods make the bulk of the merchandise. Among the good deals were single bed cotton bed sets for just £20, cheap and cheerful aluminium pans from just £6.99 and household cleaning materials for just £1. The DIY stalls are also very good value with lots of deals on smaller items – no doubt in the hope of luring punters into buying the larger items such as meter long spirit levels for £25. Wembley Stadium has its fair share of miked-up auctioneers offering electronics goods like cameras for ridiculous prices like £1 and promising to offer a full refund if you are not entirely satisfied. Having experienced childhood disappointment here I prefer to watch the free show. Another free entertainment are the numerous CD stalls playing their R&B, Soul and Dance music and trying to enjoy themselves while doing a bit of business. One stallholder took things a little further by donning a green wig and dancing on his table while his customers largely ignored him and sifted through the CDs on display.

Wembley Stadium isn't one of the best places to visit for grocery shopping, but the few fruit and veg stalls are large concerns offering bargains like six nectarines for £1 and ten oranges for the same price. The several meat stalls scattered around the market likewise offer some great deals with meaty essentials like pork, beef and lamb all sold at well below High Street prices.

Parking space is limited around the market and it is a lot easier to use the tube – Wembley Park station is just five minutes away. Events at the stadium sometime prevent the market from taking place, so it's a good idea to check on the *Wendy Fairs* website to avoid a wasted journey.

Refreshment

There is an artery clogging selection of burger and doughnut stalls at Wembley Stadium Market. If you want something a little different there is a central eating area with stalls offering food from around the world, including several Indian food stalls serving fresh naan breads and spitting kebab sticks.

Getting a Stall

For further details about getting a stall contact *Wendy Fairs* on 01895 632 221.

Willesden

Car park between Church Road and High Road, NW10
Tube: Neasden
Open: Wednesday and Saturday 8.30am-5pm

This local market takes place in a scruffy car park behind Willesden High Road. It is an important part of Willesden life in an area that seems forgotten by the rest of the Capital – certainly few visitors making their way here from outside the area.

The market offers a rare injection of commerce and activity and is always busy with locals shopping among the reasonable selection of clothing, fruit and veg, fabric, cheap packaged food, bedding and towels, household cleaning materials, bags and shoes and several R&B Cd stalls.

The people of Willesden don't seem to have too much money to throw around and the market remains popular because it offers great value on all the basics and also acts as a focal point for the community. The High Road has changed little since the war and is quiet on a Saturday afternoon while the market is busy with people shopping and stopping for a chat.

Refreshment
There are few welcoming cafés in the area, but the market does have a very good Halal Kebab stall offering delicious kebabs cooked to order.

Getting a Stall
For further details contact *Sherman Waterman Associates Ltd* who can be reached on 020 7240 7405.

west

Bayswater Road & Piccadilly

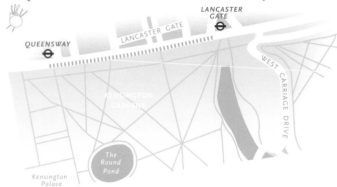

South side of Bayswater Road from Lancaster Gate to Queensway and south side of Piccadilly from Queen's Walk to Hyde Park Corner, W2 & W1

Tube: Lancaster Gate, Marble Arch (Central),
Green Park (Victoria, Piccadilly and Jubilee)
Open: Sunday 9.30am-4pm (Piccadilly & Bayswater Road), Saturday
9.30am-4pm (Piccadilly)

These two open air art markets in central London are a great place to stroll on a Sunday. Start at the Piccadilly Market then walk through Hyde Park to reach the Bayswater Market – a journey that will take about 25 minutes. Serious art buyers will find few items of interest, but for browsing the markets are great. They are almost like an outdoor art gallery (if you can ignore the touristy souvenir stalls), but minus the pretension and, occasionally without the artistry. Piccadilly Market once extended all the way along the road but these days it peters out long before Hyde Park Corner with only about thirty spaces taken at the weekend. Bayswater is larger and more vibrant on a Sunday, but even this market has been affected, with trading now only starting at Lancaster Gate when it used to extend several hundred meters further along the road.

Most of the artists are on hand to sell their paintings, and many of them take credit cards. This is a sophisticated market, even though its wares are largely aimed at tourists. All styles of painting are covered from Renaissance to Pop Art. Tourists have a wealth of schlock from which to choose including Oxford sweatshirts, London T-shirts and key rings and refrigerator magnets with emblems of the capital. For teenagers on holiday, there are plenty of stalls at the Green Park station

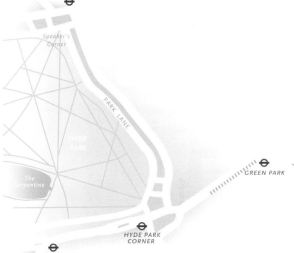

end of Piccadilly Market selling mass-produced silver and leather jewellery from Asia and bright coloured hairbands and beads. For those on a tight budget there are mini prints with magnets on the back for just £2 each and plenty of miniature paintings depicting London for around £10. Also at the Green Park station end of Piccadilly are pub towels, beer coasters and plenty of satirical prints about British life. Souvenir-style paintings depicting 19th-century London street scenes are particularly popular on Piccadilly Market and there are an equal number portraying the English countryside with subjects like canals, cows and the not to be missed 'mice in a cornfield'.

The many animal paintings (both oil and watercolour) range from elephants and lions to hens and horses with a significant number of artists devoting themselves to portraying the different breeds of dogs and cats. Cityscapes (London to New York), seascapes (with plenty of tropical beach scenes) and landscapes (from battles to Turneresque renderings) are all strongly represented – the only thing there isn't is an escape.

One of the busiest stalls sells pictures of famous London scenes made from clock parts with a working clock incorporated into the design – Big Ben is an obvious favourite for this unusual art form. Most of the vendors advertise in more than one language and will pack up paintings to be shipped abroad – more evidence that this market is not geared for native Londoners.

The Bayswater market has reduced in size in recent years, but on a Sunday it is by far the larger of the two markets. There are plenty of portrait artists here depicting Native Americans, iconic Americans

like Marilyn Monroe and Woody Allen and famous Brits like David Beckham. Landscapes here tend to be restricted to either Greek or Spanish villages, tropical beach scenes or romantic paintings of women sleeping in groves, on balconies, under trees, etc. If you want something a little more personal there is an artist who makes personalised birth and wedding announcements and is particularly in demand for her children's name plates. There is more modern art on Bayswater Road with plenty of vibrant squares of colour and abstract paintings. Of course, there are also some weird pieces too, such as the Disney characters painted on papyrus and oil paintings of modern airline jets.

It is easy to make fun of the art displayed on Bayswater and Piccadilly at the weekend, but among all the derivative stuff there are quite a few genuine artists. One artist sells his work under the name 'Gallery 235', and has established a website (www.gallery235.co.uk) to promote his sinister black ink drawings. Another regular was keen to show me his colourful paintings of the Kent coast of which he was rightly proud. Walking along the pavements talking with the artists and occasionally finding something that grabs your interest is a great way to spend a couple of hours on a Sunday and long may it continue – provided Westminster Council don't get too greedy with their rents.

Refreshment

The opposite side of Piccadilly has plenty of cafés including *Citrus Café* which is part of *Park Lane Hotel*, *Pret a Manger* and a branch of *Starbucks*. If you fancy a pint the *Rose & Crown* is a traditional pub located just behind the *Hard Rock Café*. If you're looking for something to eat on Bayswater Market *Lo Spuntino* is a popular café on the junction with Queensway and there are plenty more eateries on Queensway itself.

Local Attractions

Hyde Park has lots of things to offer including boating on the Serpentine or just having a cuppa from one of the cafés while watching the world go by. On a Sunday there is always the appeal of Speakers Corner where members of the public are encouraged to get on their soap box. If you have not tired of art there is always the *Royal Academy* on Piccadilly which is particularly good if the weather turns nasty.

Getting a Stall

For further details, contact Westminster City Council (see appendix).

Hammersmith Road

Hammersmith Grove, between King Street & Beadon Road, W6
Tube: Hammersmith (Hammersmith & City, Piccadilly and District)
Open: Thursday 10am-3pm, First and Third Saturday of every month 10am-3pm

There has been a regular weekday market in Hammersmith for over a hundred years, but the last thirty years has witnessed the market's gradual decline as old traders have retired and the next generation decided that selling fruit and veg from a stall is not for them. When I last visited the market in 2004 the number of stalls had dwindled to just three and old favourites like John Tydeman's fish stall had disappeared after over 100 years of trading.

There is now a Thursday market selling largely take-away food for the local office workers which is popular and a quality food market on the first and third Saturdays of the month. The markets are run by an organisation called *City and Country Farmers' Markets*, see the Farmers' Markets section of the book (page 228). Hammersmith is also the venue for a French market which is always popular when it occasionally takes place (see page 236 for further details).

It is very sad that the traditional market has now closed, but the new farmers' market and occasional French market are at least a small compensation for the loss and give some variety to an area dominated by dull chain stores.

North End Road

East side of North End Rd, from Walham Grove to Lillie Rd, SW6
Tube: Fulham Broadway (District)
Open: Monday-Saturday 7am-5pm, Thursday 7am-1pm (Saturday busiest day)

Fulham is one of the smarter parts of London, but the area north of Fulham Broadway forms a rectangle of ordinary streets and estates amid the wealth of West London. North End Road reflects this contrast, starting off relatively classy but becoming more and more scruffy as you head north. Recent changes to the Fulham Broadway end of the road have only increased this contrast with the pedestrian shopping area just off Fulham Broadway now redeveloped with several smart shops and cafés.

North End Road is still a good market which attracts reasonable business during the week, but is at its most exciting on a Saturday when the full contingent of stalls extends along the east side of the road between Lillie Road and Waltham Grove. It caters for mainly everyday needs from fruit and veg to carpets and pet-care accessories with the odd ultra-specialist stall such as the one selling Hoover bags. Cyril has been selling flowers on the corner of Racton Road for over 60 years and has seen the market decline from its glory days after the war. He still manages to serve his customers with a smile and offer the occasional bit of advice. Another long established favourite on the market is the fresh fish stall which offers a good range of quality fresh fish and is always busy at the weekends. The egg stall is also worth a visit with farm fresh eggs and unusual things like huge goose eggs which you won't find at any supermarket.

94

The fruit and veg stalls are the most prominent feature of the market with lots of competition among the traders. Some of the best stalls still make the effort with old-fashioned displays of regimented pears and apples sitting pertly on pink tissue paper. Jeff's fruit and veg pitch occupies a central location on the market and is one of the most popular. The stall has been in the family for several generations and Jeff continues to trade here six days a week just like his father and grandfather.

The cheap fashion clothing, underwear and small electrical goods don't have the same history at the market but still seem to attract reasonable business at the weekend. One trader offers a selection of bright summer dresses for just £4.99 a garment and is always busy dealing with the small crowd of women sifting through the stock in search of a bargain. The shoe stall is also good value with lots of quality leather footwear for £15-25 and even provides a stool for you to try the shoes before buying, which is unusual for a market stall. The leather bag dealer is also very good value with a selection of Italian leather handbags for £14-28 – which is as cheap as you'll find anywhere in London.

The arrival of two deli stalls on North End Road in recent years has greatly added to the market's appeal. The independent deli stall is only at the northern end of the street on a Saturday while the professional looking trailer sets up at the southern end of the market from Thursday to Saturday. Both stalls offer excellent quality cheeses and prepared meats. It's great to see the market adapt to the more affluent local residents who are quite willing to shop at the local market as long as the camembert is ripe and the olive oil extra virgin.

Refreshment

At number 348 is *The Café Fish Bar* which has been serving fish and chips here for over thirty years. If you fancy a pint *The Cock & Hen* is a traditional public house at the southern end of the street. A branch of *Café Nero* has established itself on the street in recent years and further south in the new pedestrian area is the very popular *Café Blue*.

Local Attractions

North End Road has several good charity shops which are worth taking a visit if you are interested in second-hand bargains.

Getting a Stall

For further details contact Hammersmith & Fulham Council (see appendix)

Portobello, W11

Portobello Road from (and including) Golborne Road to Chepstow Villas, W11

Tube: Notting Hill Gate (Central, Circle or District), Ladbroke Grove (Hammersmith & City)
Open: Monday-Wednesday, Friday-Saturday 8am-6.30pm, Thursday 8am-1pm (general market);
Friday 8am-5pm, Saturday 6am-5.30pm (Antiques), Friday-Sunday 8am-5.30pm (Portobello Green – under Westway), Mon-Sat 9am-5pm (Golborne Road)

"...the best and oddest market for antiques in London..." V.S. Pritchett

Shopping is possible on Portobello Road all week, but the market is famous for its Saturday antiques market. Antiques have been sold here since the 18th century and the tradition is still going strong with over 800 antique dealers showing up here on a Saturday and tens of thousands of tourists joining the noisy procession along the road. On a busy Saturday it is possible to walk one hundred meters and hear languages from around the world – many of them by people who live in the area, because Portobello is home to several immigrant communities who have added a little of their own flavour to the mix of food, clothing, bric-à-brac and antiques to be found along this winding road.

The southern end of the market definitely caters to a more upmarket crowd with its genuine antiques and as you head north, the goods become more modern, less posh and, perhaps, more interesting. Although there is a pocket of stalls selling collectables under the Westway which bucks this trend. If you're looking for the next big fashion trend, the northern end is a good place to start as many young designers hawk their creative wares under the vast white canopy that forms part of what is called Portobello Green Market.

Portobello Market extends for well over a mile on a Saturday and the review for the market is divided into six sections to give a detailed account of how the market transforms itself from vast upmarket antiques market in the south to a small collection of food and bric-à-brac stalls at the northern end on Golborne Road. If you want the whole Portobello experience then Saturday is the only day to visit when all parts of the market are going at full tilt, but Friday can also be a lot of fun with less antiques but also a lot less tourists. Even the flea market under the canopy can be a great way to spend a relaxing Sunday morning when the rest of the market is closed. If you like food shopping then the weekday market which takes place between Lonsdale and Lancaster Road is a great a place to spend a few hours. Portobello is one of London's most famous markets and continues to be one of the best.

Portobello

Chepstow Villas to Lonsdale Road
(antiques and collectables)

This is the first part of Portobello Market when approaching from Notting Hill tube station, but the place is quiet throughout the week with just a handful of antique stalls showing up on a Friday. It is on Saturdays that the area from Chepstow Villas to Lonsdale Road is transformed into London's largest antiques market with over 200 stalls trading on the pavement and many more from the numerous indoor markets that lie along this stretch of quaint 19th century shop fronts. There are all manner of antiques and collectables to be found here from rare and expensive items of silverware and crystal to more quirky stalls selling cheap bric-à-brac for just a few pounds. Among the specialist dealers is Vicky Sleeper who has been selling her fine collection of vintage handbags and luggage from her stall outside the *Admiral Vernon* for many years and still enjoys the hustle and bustle of the market. A nearby stall is doing a roaring trade in old jewellery with lots of things piled up on the stall for just £1 and the best pieces sold for the princely sum of just £4. *The Chelsea Galleries* (stall enquiries: 0207 733 3761) at no. 67, 69, and 73 has plenty of dealers selling porcelain, glass, silver and jewellery and has a café upstairs if you feel in need of a rest. Where Portobello meets Westbourne Road, the *Good Fairy Antique Market* (www.goodfairyantiques.co.uk) has about 50 stalls selling jewellery, accessories, and silver. Across the road is the first indoor market to be established on Portobello Road, *Roger's Antiques Gallery* (stall enquiries: 07887 527 523), which is still going strong with over 80 dealers. Farther along is the *Admiral Vernon Antique Market* at no. 141-149 (stall enquiries: 020 7727 5240) where there are hundreds of dealers as well as a café. Lonsdale Road is basically the finishing point for the antiques traders even though a few stragglers can be found beyond this point.

Lonsdale Road to Lancaster Road
(Food, flowers and clothing)

The antiques market peters out at the junction with Lonsdale Road and is replaced by an assortment of food and new fashion stalls. While the clothing is reasonable quality street fashion the real appeal of this part of Portobello is the excellent food. There are all kinds of fruit and veg to be found here from basics to more exotic produce catering for the varied cultural mix of the area with yams and cassava displayed alongside fresh limes and coriander. The stalls vary in style from the elaborate to the more mundane, but the quality and freshness of the produce is high throughout, helped by the busy crowds and high turnover. Accompanying the fruit and veg stalls are several long established fresh fish stalls which are doing well judging by the empty display units and big smiles on a Saturday afternoon. Portobello is the kind of market where you can do a complete shop at the weekend with several deli stalls offering fine cheeses and prepared meats and a choice of good bread stalls which not only offer fresh baked breads but also tempting pastries and cakes.

Refreshment

If all this food has made you peckish there are lots of fast food stalls on the market including the German Sausage stall which is a long established feature of the market and can easily be found by following the delicious smell. Visitors to the market with an interest in food should look out for *Books for Cooks* on Blenheim Crescent. It is the only specialist cookbook shop in London and also has a wonderful café at the back. Another good place for a coffee is *The Tea and Coffee Plant* (180 Portobello Road) which sells fresh coffee as well as making a mean cappuccino.

Lancaster Road to the Westway
(New Clothing and household goods)

Here the market concentrates on the kind of new clothes and household goods to be found at most local markets. The goods are not very inspirational but there are enough good quality designer copies to make the area worth a gander. Handbags, watches, fabric, scarves and trainers are all up for grabs along this stretch of the market. Occasionally, you might just find something of interest amid the dross. The shops behind the stalls are mix of hippy wares and products for hip clubbers.

Old Spitalfields Market

Commercial Street
London E1
020 7247 8556

Nearest Tubes
Liverpool St/Aldgate
Open
Thursday
Antiques & Vintage
Friday
Fashion, Arts & Crafts
Sunday
The Full Market

Portobello Green Market

'Under the Westway'
Portobello Road
London W10
0800 358 3434

Nearest Tubes
Ladbroke Grove/
Notting Hill Gate
Open
Friday
Fashion & Vintage
Saturday
The Full Market
Sunday
Bric-a-Brac

Une Normande à Londres

www.unenormandealondres.co.uk

Acton Market
Market Place, W3
(sun)

Regent's Park Road, NW1
(sun)

Chapel Market, N1
(fri-sat-sunday)

Duke of York Square, SW3
Chelsea
(sat)

Portobello Road, W11
(opp. Electric Cinema)
(fri-sat)

North End Road, SW6
(corner of Walham Grove)
(fri-sat)

Hampstead Community
Centre, NW3
(sat)

Brick Lane, E1
(Bacon Street)
(sun)

Leadenhall market, EC3
(fri)

Borough Market, SE1
Green Market
(fri-sat)

French Cheeses in London

Portobello Green

Under the Westway and west up to Ladbroke Grove
(Retro and new clothing, CDs and records, books and collectables)

The Westway flyover marks the beginning of a funkier and more entertaining part of the market. This is a glimpse of Notting Hill before the gentrification and before the media hype changed the area beyond recognition. Walking up from Notting Hill on your left is an indoor shopping area with lots of interesting independent shops and from Friday to Saturday you will find a choice of about 30 antiques and collectables dealers selling all kinds of jewellery, bric-à-brac and things for the home with quite a few bargains to be found. Just a few metres further on the market splits with a less formal selection of bric-à-brac and retro clothing stalls to the right. This area becomes increasingly chaotic the further from Portobello Road you walk, beginning with excellent retro clothing stalls including one which takes the time to display the smart men's suits on manikins. Such niceties gradually disappear further along as clothes are sold in piles for just a few pounds. The market ends with a few pitches selling an assortment of things from blankets on the pavement. On the other side of Portobello Road is a large white awning under which over 60 retro clothing stalls and independent designers ply their trade. This is the best part of the market for retro clothing with lots of choice and plenty of bargains and there are always good bric-à-brac stalls, particularly on a Sunday when the rest of the market is closed.

Refreshment

Just beyond the Westway is *Falafel King* (274 Portobello Road) which serves great food and has seating outside on fine days. A little further along are three eateries *Uncles*, *Thai Rice* and *Santo*, which are next to each other and are worth a try.

Getting a Stall

The area of the market under the Westway is privately run, call 020 8962 5724 for further details.

Portobello Road from Acklam Road to Golborne Road

(Retro and new clothing, bric-à-brac, furniture and electrical goods)

This final stretch of Portobello Road leading up to Golborne Road used to be almost entirely dedicated to second-hand clothing and bric-à-brac, but has undergone a considerable change in recent years. These days there is a lot more new clothing on the road and only a handful of the second-hand dealers. Steve has been selling an assortment of old pictures and collectables every Saturday for more years than he wishes to admit and still enjoys trading here. There are still some bargains to be found and the new stalls are interesting with one trader selling new trendy trainers for £30 and zip-up tops for £20. In addition there are also a few independent designers that sell here which adds to the appeal of this part of the market.

Golborne Road Market

(Junk, furniture and fruit and veg)

Running from Portobello Road to St Ervans Road, Golborne Road market is at the heart of Moroccan and Portuguese London. The area is still a little rough around the edges but there are signs of gentrification with several antique shops now established here. This a great place to escape the tourists while enjoying a bit of the Portobello Road experience in a diverse environment. On weekdays it is a local market selling fruit and veg and household goods, but on Fridays and Saturdays there are a number of traders who deal in bric-à-brac and second-hand goods with a sea of junk extending onto the pavement on fine days.

Refreshment

One of the best places for a nosh is *Lisboa Patisserie* at no. 57 serving delightful Portuguese pastries and strong coffee.

Local Attractions

Of interest to architecture enthusiasts will be the soaring Trellick Tower that hovers over the skyline here. It was designed by Erno Goldfinger in 1973 and is now a Grade-II listed building.

Getting a stall

There are two bodies running market stalls in Portobello:
a) Most of the market is run by Kensington & Chelsea Council (see Appendix)
b) The area under the Westway is privately run, call 020 8962 5724 for further details.

Shepherd's Bush

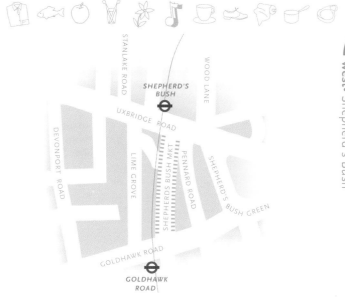

Between Uxbridge Road and Goldhawk Road W12

Tube: Shepherd's Bush, Goldhawk Road (Metropolitan)
Open: Monday-Saturday 9am-5pm, Thursday 9am-1pm

Shepherd's Bush is a remarkably mixed area. On Shepherd's Bush Green there are large pubs packed with young people drinking too much beer and watching sport while just down Goldhawk Road at the entrance to Shepherd's Bush Market, Middle-Eastern women in full Islamic dress await the arrival of their limousines to take them home. It struck me as strange that women shopping at the local market should have a limousine, but it emerged that the limos are in fact glorified taxis that turn up every ten minutes to pick up their fares.

Entering the market from Goldhawk Road it is evident that the cultural mix is even more complex with many African, Middle-Eastern, West Indian and Asian people living, shopping and trading in the area. The market also has a variety of shops, lock-ups and stalls all vying for your attention as they extend parallel to the overhead Metropolitan line with the occasional sight of a tube train to remind you that this is still London and not some foreign bazaar.

The market does not just run along the eastern side of the tube line, but also has a fairly large square and a passageway on the western side which connects to the main market via two narrow arches. It is in this smaller maze of shops that most of the specialist African food stalls are situated as well as a few selling African music along with the usual mix of street fashion, cheap shoes, bags and a few outlets selling fabric by the metre. Among some of the more interesting outlets is the excellent 101 which offers fashionable footwear at below High Street prices. Dave's Drapers is another established feature of the market selling great value fabrics for as little as £1 per metre.

The market is especially strong on fresh food, with many top-notch fruit and veg stalls ranging from those dealing in standard fare to others with more exotic produce. One such stall is located about half-way down the market and has all kinds of unusual vegetables – yams, cassava, plantain and dried pumpkin. There are also several good butchers within the market selling basics as well as more recherché things to cater for the African community such as pigs trotters and cows' tongues. Likewise there are plenty of good fresh fish stalls offering anything from smoked haddock to fresh tuna and red snapper.

Although many of the things found at Shepherd's Bush Market are unexceptional, the atmosphere and diversity of the place make it worth visiting. There are also some real bargains to be found here with cotton sheets recently on offer for only £5.99 and good quality travel bags for under £20.

Refreshment

There are several good falafel stalls along the market which reflect the culinary tastes of the Middle-Eastern locals. If you want traditional British food try *A. Cooke* pie and mash shop on Goldhawk Road.

Getting a Stall

The market is run by London Transport and there are all kinds of pitches available, for more details phone 020 7918 4067.

Southwest

Battersea High Street

South end of Battersea High Street, up to the junction with Simpson Road, SW11

Rail: Clapham Junction (Victoria, Waterloo)
Open: Saturday 9.30am-4.30pm

In its Victorian heyday Battersea High Street was the venue for a huge and vibrant street market that supplied the local community with all its shopping requirements throughout the week. The market was still trading on weekdays until about 25 years ago, but even then it was a shadow of its former self. These days it has dwindled to just five stalls that show up on a Saturday to offer the locals a reasonable selection of fruit and veg, pet food and accessories, fresh meat, household goods, street fashion and flowers.

Battersea is not the only local market to suffer this fate, with Hammersmith and Hildreth Street both declining in recent years. There have been attempts to get a Farmers' Market going on the street, but the residents of Battersea didn't shop there and it has now ceased trading for the present.

Refreshment

Jack Hall Dining Rooms is a defiantly old fashioned caff which still serves a good cup of tea and offers traditional grub like Spotted Dick and Treacle Pudding. For a more contemporary dining experience try *Chez Manny*, at the far end of the street. *The Galapagos Deli* now has a café with seating but still offers great take-away food.

Brixton Market

a) Brixton Village
b) Market Row
c) Reliance Arcade
d) Tunstall Road (Arts & Crafts)

Brixton Station Road, Pope's Road, Atlantic Road, Electric Road and Electric Avenue, SW9

Tube/Rail: Brixton (Victoria Line)
Open: Monday-Saturday 8am-5.30pm, Wednesday 8am-1pm
Tunstall Road (arts & crafts) Saturday 9am-5pm

Brixton was a smart place one hundred years ago and there are still signs of its Edwardian grandeur in some of the architecture, particularly along Electric Avenue (which was one of the first streets to have electricity in the 1870's). The area was in decline for many years but took on a new lease of life when West Indians settled here after the war and Brixton Market adapted to cater for the new comers with lots of stalls offering exotic fabrics and unusual ingredients joining the usual array of household goods and everyday fruit and veg.

These days Brixton market has a run-down appearance and the large arcades that form a significant part of the market are certainly in need of renovation. The council are taking some measures to improve the situation with Pope's Road being smartened up, but there is still a great deal to be done to restore some of Brixton's Edwardian charm. The market is still a great place to shop for food amid the sprawling mix of roads, arcades and railway arches. The experience can be a bit disorientating, but there are plenty of watering holes for those who need to stop and get their bearings.

Electric Avenue

This is one of the main thoroughfares of the market and a great place to start if your interest is food shopping. There are lots of excellent fruit and veg stalls here, as well as a top-notch fishmonger and butcher to complement the market. Near the junction with Atlantic Road there's a very good Thai supermarket emphasising Brixton's cultural and culinary diversity. Food isn't the only thing on offer here and there are a number of stalls selling consumer durables like street fashion, jewellery, bedding and towels, fabric by the yard, household goods, bags, accessories and watches. It's worth raising your eyes from the market to take notice of the rather grand architecture that curves above the functional shop fronts, giving some clue to Brixton's past prosperity.

Pope's Road

This road leads on from Electric Avenue, but has none of its charm. In place of grand architecture there is an ugly Iceland supermarket and the road seems something of an afterthought. The council has recently made efforts to improve things with smart new pavements being laid to give the area a face lift. In terms of the market there are quite a few quality fruit and veg stalls as well as cheap fashion and shoes, kids' clothing, small electrical goods, bedding, kitchenware and one specialising in cheap plastic toys. One of the entrances to Brixton Village is on Pope's Road.

Brixton Station Road

This part of Brixton used to be renowned for the number and diversity of its second-hand stalls and shops trading from the railway arches. The numbers have dwindled in the last ten years and now all the second-hand stalls have disappeared and only one of the permanent lock-ups is still trading. On the corner of Brixton Road there are a handful of stalls selling new clothing, fruit and veg and CDs, but that is all that remains of the market on this now quiet back street.

Refreshment

The Portuguese café, *Max Snack Bar*, is a popular local eatery and there are also several kiosks serving Caribbean and Indian food.

LEMON &TENT
30p
Each
4 for 1=

©Brixton Market

Brixton Village

Although this is the largest arcade in Brixton Market it's surprisingly bright and airy with plenty of skylights and light-coloured walls. There are quite a few stalls stocking household goods, but this is a particularly good place to find exotic foods with many stalls selling Afro-Caribbean spices and flavourings, several good fishmongers and greengrocers, as well as stalls specialising in Chinese and Asian ingredients. Although the main avenue is busy, the rest of the place is quiet, with lots of vacant units among the handful of struggling traders. The grand Victorian structure is now looking tatty and could certainly do with a lick of paint, but such things cost money and little of the stuff is flowing into this market at the moment.

Brixton Market

Market Row

This indoor arcade between Atlantic Road and Electric Lane has high ceilings and plenty of natural light making it a pleasant place to shop. Among the units there is a reasonable selection of fruit and veg, street fashion, fresh fish, household goods, fabric by the meter and toiletries. *Dombey Wholesale Butchers* is one of the major attractions of the market and usually has a queue of people at the weekend. A recent welcome addition is the new bakery – the only one in the area to bake on site, and an indication that this arcade is on the up.

Reliance Arcade

This narrow passageway is darker than the other arcades in the market and has only a handful of stalls offering kid's clothes and Christian iconography as well as being home to an excellent music outlet.

Tunstall Road (Arts & Crafts Market)

This Saturday market has about ten regular stalls offering a mix of music CDs, new clothing, jewellery and flowers. The market is crammed into a small side street just off Brixton Road, and gets a lot of passing trade being just next door to Body Shop.

Refreshments

There are several good places to eat within the Brixton Village, including an excellent Columbian café and a West Indian eatery called *Take Zwo*.

Market Row has several great places to eat including the fabulous *Rosie's Deli Café* and a smart new pizzeria called *Franca Manca*. For more basic fare there is also *Eser Café*.

Getting a Stall

For further details about getting a stall contact Brixton Market Office on 020 7926 2530.

Broadway & Tooting

a) Broadway Market
b) Tooting Market

Broadway, SW17

Upper Tooting Road
Tube: Tooting Broadway (Northern)
Open: Monday-Saturday 9.30am-5pm, Wednesday until 1pm

This covered market doesn't promise much from the street (the entrance nearest the tube is a gap between tacky shops leading into a dingy passage), but Broadway Market is certainly worth a look. The lack of steady trade and a tendency towards half-hearted presentation make it a bit underwhelming in terms of atmosphere, but the mixture of standard utility goods and services aimed at the local Afro-Caribbean and Asian communities means there are plenty of cheap and interesting things to buy if you take time to explore.

Afro-Caribbean food and vegetables are well-stocked and supplemented by meat, seafood and fish stalls which are all impressively cheap. There is also an excellent fruit and veg stall at the very back of the market, which has people queuing for the veggie bargains. The rest of the market offers lots of choice on household goods, stationery, underwear, luggage and cosmetics. Fabric, haberdashery, Indian jewellery and accessories also get units to themselves so, for keen dressmakers, there's the possibility of knocking up endless ritzy outfits on the cheap. Other than the unit selling colourful kids' separates in the main square, the clothes on offer are pretty forgettable.

In amongst all this are specialist traders selling more unusual goods like African wood crafts, African batik and novelty balloons: order a while-you-wait balloon-twist giraffe for 50p. Broadway Market's nail salon can send you all Beverley Hills with glued on individual diamanté stars for 50p. The other unit worth a look is the fish and pet stall, which has tanks set up like an aquatic video wall, plus an impressive selection of kitschy fish accessories, plastic pond plants and general pet supplies.

Refreshment
Fill up on something from the small Afro-Caribbean take-away or go next door to Tooting Market which has a much more lively café. There is also *Harrington's* pie and mash shop, just across the way on Selkirk Road. Tooting is also a good place for a curry, with *Lahore Karahi* (1 Tooting High Street) being among the best.

Getting a Stall
For further details contact the Market Office on 020 8672 6613.

Tooting SW17
Upper Tooting Road
Tube: Tooting Broadway (Northern)
Open: Monday-Saturday 9.30am-5pm, Wednesday until 1pm
A few yards further along Upper Tooting Road from Broadway Market is Tooting Market, it's slightly smaller but livelier twin. Essentially this L-shaped covered market covers the same sort of territory, with a range of utilitarian units enlivened by the odd unexpected specialist. Meat and fruit and veg are well covered with the fruit and veg stall at the entrance being by far the most popular feature of the market.

The Afro-Caribbean influence is strong, with a large grocery shop in the far corner selling many varieties of exotic vegetables. The *Vallo Oriental Shop* makes the choice of food even more international with every imaginable noodle and cooking sauce, as well as a great selection of herbs, teas (good quality oolong and jasmine leaf tea are cheap) and unusual canned beans and vegetables at well below supermarket prices.

In amongst the remainder of the stalls there are a few other noteworthy units including the old man who sells second-hand fixtures, fittings and tools from a small unit with bargains like antique brass door knockers for £10. The old fashioned tobacconist at the entrance to the market has now gone to be replaced by a dealer in mobile phone accessories – a sign of the times.

Hildreth Street

Hildreth Street, SW12
Tube: Balham (Northern)
Rail: Balham
Open: Monday-Saturday 9.30am-5pm, Wednesdays until 1pm

Hildreth Street market has been located in this pedestrianised corridor between grand Toblerone-roofed Victorian buildings since the turn of the century, but has now declined to just two regular stalls offering cut flowers and an excellent range of fruit and veg. It is really sad to see a market decline like this but the local community seem to prefer shopping in the nearby Sainsbury's and that, above all, is the reason for the market's gradual decline.

The demise of Hildreth Street is a great pity because the venue is perfect for a market. The council have even invested in new pavements and a large metal gateway above the pedestrian walkway declaring 'Hildreth Street Market' – which now seems almost ironic with only two traders showing up here. A farmers' market did trade on Sundays for a while, but the locals gradually lost interest and the venture closed in 2007. The council still have ambitions for the market, but no concrete plans are currently under consideration.

Getting a Stall
For further details contact Wandsworth Council (see appendix).

Merton Abbey Mills

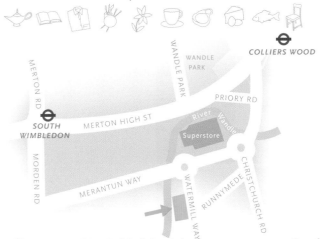

Off Merantun Way, Behind the Sainsburys superstore, South Wimbledon, SW19

Tube: Colliers Wood (Northern)
Open: Saturday-Sunday 10am-5pm,

Merton Abbey Mills started life as workshops for artisans and became associated with William Morris's *Arts and Crafts Movement* which attempted to buck the trend towards mass production in favour of handcrafted quality goods. The movement died out long ago but the group of buildings including the 18th century Watermill and Colourhouse are still there to be explored. In 1989 the site was restored and transformed into the location for a weekend market with cafés and permanent shops. In the last few years there has been considerable building work going on around the market which is now finished, but seems to have had a considerable effect on the market with the loss of many stalls and several of the most interesting shops.

Walking along Merton High Street from Colliers Wood tube station, ignore the signs that direct you through the modern shopping centre to the market and instead take the footpath alongside the river Wandle. The river is a very important part of the history of Merton Abbey Mills and provides a much more attractive route to the market than the sterile atmosphere of an indoor shopping centre. The market goes to some lengths to entertain visitors with live music regularly performed at the bandstand and lots of things such as face painting and a bouncy castle to keep the smaller ones amused.

The uncommon Market
MERTON ABBEY MILLS

Wimbledon's Unique Riverside Centre

Market every Saturday & Sunday 10-5

Arts, Crafts & Gifts
Fresh Farm Produce
Children's Theatre
Wheelhouse Museum and Potterys

Shops, Restaurants & Pub open all week

From Wimbledon Station: buses 57 & 200 to Merton Bus Garage
Nearest tube Colliers Wood - plenty of free parking, Tel: 020 8543 9608

The market has about 30 stalls setting up here at the weekend offering a variety of things from top quality food to clothing and gifts. Keith Cook runs the food stall at the market and has established a loyal following of customers looking for farm fresh produce including Scottish beef, farm fresh sausages and a delicious range of meats and cheeses from Denhay Farm in Dorset. The olive oil stall in the main thoroughfare is another regular feature of the market offering a unique extra virgin brand sourced direct from a single producer. The market has lost a great many of its fashion stalls in recent years but Sue has remained loyal to the market and continues to offer a good selection new and vintage women's dresses for between £15 and £30. Other stalls worthy of mention include a milliner making her own range of colourful hats, an excellent haberdashers stall and Frank, who sells a range of quality garden furniture and mirrors. Sadly, the Long Shop is being developed into permanent units and all the craft stalls have been moved into a tent where the usual assortment of scented candles, contemporary art and jewellery can be found.

Merton Abbey has always been one of those markets that is on the verge of becoming a real success, but has never quite made the transition. Other more successful markets like Spitalfields and the Stables Market in Camden have experienced upheaval and redevelopment and emerged undamaged and vibrant. Merton Abbey Mills has experienced a more dramatic turn down in business and it is hoped that it can regain its momentum in the years to come.

Refreshment

The *Commonwealth Café* is a great place to go for coffee and snacks and has plenty of seating both inside and out. The massive pizza restaurant on site is very handy if you want a meal and there is also the *William Morris* free house towards the back of the market if you fancy a pint. A permanent block of three cafés has been built next to the Long Shop and these offer further places to get a bite to eat and relax.

Getting a Stall

For further details about a stall phone 020 8543 9608.

Merton Abbey Mills

Nine Elms Sunday Market, SW8

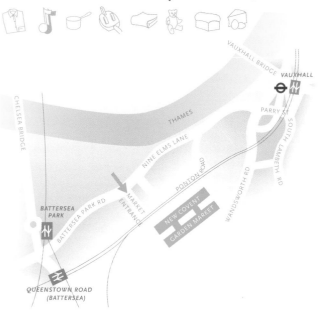

The market is sited inside New Covent Garden Market, but on a Sunday, pedestrians can't access it through the flower market complex to the north. The easiest way to get in is to follow Nine Elms Lane south for about 10 minutes, and then turn into the market's access road when you reach the Booker Cash & Carry depot on your left.

Rail: Battersea Park

Open: Sunday 9am-2pm

Nine Elms market offers the sort of utility classics that street markets do best, plus a lively atmosphere and plenty of decent bric-à-brac to pick over on the car-boot stalls which share its pitch space. The problem is its location, in the central row of what during the week is New Covent Garden vegetable market. Gaining access to Nine Elms can, for pedestrians, feel like trying to pick your way across a cross-channel freight depot. Once you've slogged up the access road, through the underpass, across a slip road and found a gap in the car park wall, then shimmied between a few lorry bumpers and located the right access arch – the sight of human life inside the market comes as a real relief.

There is no shortage of life inside the market as tides of people move round the large circuit of stalls in a rough-and-ready atmosphere, stoked by loud music stalls and the fairground waft of fast-food vans. Nine Elms offers no real suprises, about half the stalls sell new clothes and shoes while the remainder offer standard market clobber including kitchenware, bedding, toys, fake flowers, plants, plastic bits and pieces, towels and some fairly dodgy ornaments. The clothes are incredibly cheap, with nothing much over £5. The catch is the quality. You might get the odd bargain on a pair of trainers or Birkenstock-style sandals, but there's not much to tempt anyone after something to wear from the ankles up. The ranges seem to concentrate on either mumsy dresses or skimpy teen fashions. But as with all markets, the piles of boxer shorts, ladies' underwear and socks are worth a rummage for cheap and cheerful cotton staples.

Ironically, although New Covent Garden is one of the country's largest fruit and veg wholesale markets there is only a limited range of veg on a Sunday. What is available is good value with lots of fruit and veg sold by the box or large bag for just a few quid. Epicures will find little of appeal, but there is one stallholder selling a range of interesting-looking Mediterranean cheeses. Nine Elms also has a good selection of DIY stalls that offer serious reductions on bewildering arrays of vital tools and gismos. The CD stall has a surprisingly broad and up-to-date range of music, selling chart titles for just £10. Also have a look at the car-boot pitches to the right of the entrance. Although much of the stuff on sale is only a whisker away from being skip fodder, there are a few people offering decent retro kitchenware, clocks and small bits of furniture.

Refreshment

If you don't fancy an old-school burger or hot-dog then you could try the *Market Café* for a no-frills greasy brunch. .

Local Attractions

Battersea Park is one of London's largest and grandest parks and is only ten minutes walk from the market..

Getting a Stall

For more details contact Group Geraud on 0151 233 2165.

Northcote Road

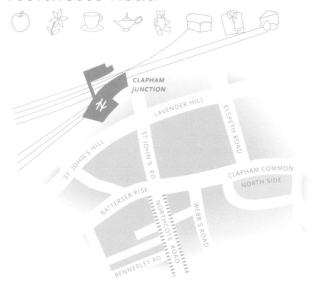

North end of Northcote Road, SW11

Rail: Clapham Junction (Victoria, Waterloo)

Open: Monday–Saturday 9am–5pm, Wednesday 9am–1pm

Northcote Road has undergone something of a revolution in the last decade. What was once an ordinary market street is now a bustling strip of slick shops and eateries which are a focus for SW11's smart set. The transformation of the area with the arrival of smart deli's and gift shops on a tidal wave of cappuccino froth was initially a bad thing for the old street market, but over the years the market has adapted to the changes. It is now thriving – particularly on a Friday and Saturday when a good mix of clothing, food, gifts and furniture stretches from Bennerley Road to just after Cairns Road. The market continues to prosper with one or two new arrivals in recent years and several of the stalls extending their trading throughout the week.

The fruit and veg traders around Mallinson Road form the heart of the market and are the longest serving pitches, trading from ancient wooden stalls which have been in the same family for several generations, although the traders of the past would probably be a bit baffled by the artichokes, asparagus, celeriac and oyster mushrooms which are now regularly on display here. The fruit and veg dealers are

Northcote Road

now kept company by a range of stalls catering for the new denizens of SW11. The photographer displaying a selection of his black and white photographs of London scenes is now an established feature of the market and close by is the fashion stall 'Maramalade Made' which offers well chosen women's fashion for around £45 a garment from its brightly decorated stall which is here on Fridays and Saturdays.

On the junction with Mallinson Road is one of the best flower and plant stalls to be found anywhere in London with lots of wonderful cut flowers and an unusually wide choice of garden herbs. Proceeding further north there are more stalls that exemplify the market's transformation in recent years. The stall offering wood furniture and antiques has been here for several years and has made a surprising success of selling solid wooden chests for as much as £250. On the corner of Shelgate Road is a large display of bread and pastry, but again the slant is towards a moneyed clientele with chiabatta and almond croissant to the fore. It would be easy to dismiss these stalls as catering for yuppies, but it's difficult to complain with a mouth full of fresh croissant.

Another sign that this market is on the up is the arrival of a good quality fishmongers which now has a place on the corner of Shelgate Road. Northcote Road Fisheries ran a shop here for many years but, with rising rents, decided to trade from the market and now sell here throughout the week. The jewellery dealer has also decorated her stall and offers a range of jewellery from as many as twelve independent designers with prices starting from a very reasonable £20 for a ring and going up to as much as £160 for an elaborate necklace. Another stalwart of the market is the flower stall near Shelgate Road which has been run by the same family for generations. The current incumbents are a friendly father and son team who are keen to dispense gardening advice and can prepared bouquets to order.

Further along is a more basic fruit and veg stall which is kept company by several fancy deli stalls with one offering olives, salads, and feta cheese from large wooden vats and the other selling a fine selection of cheeses and prepared meats. One of the best fashion stalls on the market is to be found close to Cairns Road where a good choice of independent British fashion labels are sold for between £15 and £125. For those with less money and more children there was a rail of fashionable kid's wear reduced to only £5 a garment. The market ends with the long established mirror man who offers a variety of designs and sizes for £29-£149 and even has a little dance in the street when the mood takes him.

Northcote Road is on the up with several new stalls adding to the appeal of the place and even more trading throughout the week. In the course of my research I have encountered so much despondency (some of it justified) at other markets, it is a joy to visit a place with a more positive atmosphere. It would probably benefit some market traders to visit Northcote Road on a Saturday, just to see how some stalls are adapting to modern times.

Refreshment

There are so many trendy cafés on Northcote Road that the one thing you will have no problem getting is refreshment. My favourite is the *Crumpet Coffee Shop* which does a good cappuccino and has plenty of seating. Another very popular place to eat is the *Gourmet Burger Kitchen* which does fancy burgers at an equally fancy price.

Local Attractions

There are some fantastic food shops along Northcote Road which complement the market. Among the best of these is *Hamish Johnston*, the very fine deli on the corner of Shelgate Road and the traditional butchers at the top of the market. If you like rummaging for second-hand things, there are several good charity shops on the street which, being located in such a posh area, tend to stock a better class of cast-off.

Getting a Stall

For further details contact Wandsworth Council (see appendix).

GIANT SUNDAY MARKET
WIMBLEDON GREYHOUND STADIUM
Plough Lane SW19

EVERY SUNDAY from 9am

Manager, Clive Williams: 07956 961640

WILLESDEN GENERAL MARKET
Church Road, London NW10

WEDNESDAYS AND SATURDAYS from 9am

Manager, Gary Saunders: 07831 420504

Tel: 020 7240 7405
Sherman & Waterman Associates

Wimbledon Stadium

Wimbledon Stadium car park, Plough Lane, SW19

Rail: Haydons Road

Open: (New goods) Sunday 9am-2pm;

(Car Boot Sale) Wednesday 10am-2pm and Saturday 7am-2pm

If you have an image of Wimbledon which involves manicured lawns, ivy covered buildings and strawberries and cream, then Wimbledon Stadium Market is going to be a shock. The stadium is a modern and fairly uninteresting building and is surrounded by an equally unimpressive urban landscape. About 150 stalls set up in the concrete car park alongside the stadium every Sunday, offering a wide selection of new goods and food. The only thing this market has in common with the hallowed ground of SW19, is that it also sells strawberries – although at £1.50 a large box, rather than a fiver for a small bowl.

As you enter the market your attention will be drawn to the large lorry selling cheap electronic goods. The diminutive salesman is a real pro and always has a large crowd of eager punters hanging on his every word. "Ladies and gents, take a look at this. A Goodmans flat screen telly. This top of the range piece of technology sells for over £500 on the High Street and that is not one word of a lie. I could sell you this box for half-price – just £250. Wait sir, wait, I haven't finished, put your money away! I'm not going to do that. No sir. I'm not going to sell it for £225, not £200, not £180...no, no, no. That's right madam, here today it's just £150, that right just £150. That's right, one at a time please...". I can't vouch for the apparent bargains he offers, but it's great entertainment to watch him sell.

Other things to be found at this market include cheap street fashion, all kinds of shoe, a more limited range of plants and garden ornaments, brightly coloured nylon rugs, leather jackets and bags, vacuum cleaner accessories, small electrical goods for the kitchen, DVDs, household goods and bedding. The shoe stalls were particularly impressive with several really large displays and plenty of good deals for around a tenner. The trader selling household electrics avoided any sales spiel, but had some attractive deals. There are numerous stalls flogging cheap street fashion, but much of it is dull and synthetic. Look out for pitches selling designer label copies, many of which are good quality.

Wimbledon Stadium mainly deals in consumer durables, but there are enough good food stalls to make this a market worth visiting for essentials. Carnivores are particularly well catered for with several established butchers' lorries offering ridiculously cheap deals on all kinds of meat with frozen bags of sausages and bacon going for just a fiver. There are only two fruit and veg stalls on the market but both are huge and feature some great bargains with lots of people queuing to stock up for the week at well below supermarket prices. The only exotic comestibles were found at the olive and feta cheese stall and the pitch selling dried fruits and nuts. Both stalls were quiet with the average punter here preferring basics to anything fancy. Most passers-by turned their noses up even when offered a free taster.

Those with an interest in buying second-hand clobber should visit on a Wednesday or Saturday, when the area is given over to about 80 stalls selling all kinds of second-hand gear from hi-fi equipment to bric-à-brac. See the Car Boot Sale section on page 233.

Refreshment

There are a few burgers vans on site offering teas and fried food and there is an excellent café called *Cuisine & Dreams* at the entrance to the market.

Getting a Stall

For further details contact *Sherman Waterman Associates Ltd* who can be reached on 020 7240 7405.

southeast

Bermondsey

Bermondsey Square, between Abbey Street, Bermondsey Street and Tower Bridge Street, SE1

Tube: Borough, London Bridge (Northern)
Rail: London Bridge
Open: Fridays 4am-1pm

Bermondsey Market is London's most famous antiques market and enjoys a clandestine reputation partly because the market starts trading in pre-dawn darkness at about 4am. Another reason for the market's reputation was the run-down nature of the Bermondsey area with a scruffy car park surrounded by dilapidated warehouses serving as the markets location since the Second World War. The area has undergone something of a transformation in recent years with lots of new flats being built. This transformation has engulfed Bermondsey Square and for the last three years the regular traders have kept the market running amid a building site for the construction of a new square with shops, offices, flats, cafés and a supermarket. The developers have been obliged to make accommodation for the market and since June 2008 a new square with space for up to 200 stalls has been completed.

Despite all the disruption in recent years the market has kept its focus as the centre of a very serious antiques trade with lots of buying and selling taking place by torch light and many buyers coming from abroad to pick up items for sale on the Continent. Displays encompass an almost overwhelming range of silverware, jewellery, clocks, glassware, prints, crockery and porcelain. A lot of well-informed scrutinising takes place as people pick over thousands of collectables, discuss their merits and begin the task of haggling the price down. On a recent visit a man was wandering among the stalls with his collection of antiques trying to sell them with very little success. One trader handed back a 17th Century bowl and exclaimed "Silver? Looks more like tin to me…'

Although a lot of business takes place before dawn, the market continues to trade until lunchtime and often becomes more crowded after 9 o'clock. It is during the daylight hours that a more relaxed crowd flocks to the market to stroll among the stalls in the search for antique bargains. Many of the visitors are tourists and it is worth visiting Bermondsey to witness a trader negotiating with a Japanese visitor without the aid of a common language and instead reverting to gesticulation and grunting noises of ascent or disagreement. At another stall a trader took a very much more direct approach with a curious punter, "that's fifty pounds" and when she started walking away, "do you like it, and do you have cash?" When she replied in the affirmative he closed in for the kill and managed to get £42 for a large 1930's vase. The antiques trade has a rather cut-throat reputation, but there seems to be a good deal of camaraderie at Bermondsey with traders asking each others advice about the value of a particular item and even discussing how much money they have taken.

Prices reflect the quality of the goods, with few glaring bargains jumping out from the spread of beautiful and unusual pieces. Although friendly, it's unlikely dealers will do you many favours, especially on more unique objects, but appealing items can still be picked up for under a tenner. Bargains on a recent visit included an attractive contemporary oil painting for £75, sets of silver cutlery for £7 and even some modern electronic goods with one stall offering a selection of Roberts radios for £20 each. Shopping around for the less unique items can also reduce prices significantly, so don't go for the first example of something you like – it may well be £5 cheaper on a nearby stall. The costume jewellery is particularly interesting, with a lot of exceptional pieces, for example, twenties vulcanite (a coal-based plastic) chain-link necklaces were going for around £35. It's refreshing that despite being a market full of antiques, outcrops of genuine idiosyncrasy are everywhere at Bermondsey, with old German microscopes sitting alongside collectable Dinky Toys, and a Barbie doll with her plastic chest exposed to the elements, next to a fine set of chess pieces.

Bermondsey Market has certainly had a difficult time over the last few years. The large, warren-like antique warehouses on Long Lane and Bermondsey Street have all gone and the much loved *Rose Dining Room* has closed its doors for the last time. Despite these setbacks the market has survived and looks set for better times in this new attractive site which is destined to be its home for many years to come.

Refreshment

There are several cafés planned for the new site and the regular refreshment van will continue to be a feature of the market. Further away, *Manze* on the south end of Tower Bridge Street offers an authentic pie and mash experience for around £3, but doesn't open till 10am which is a little late for early visitors to the market. Just a few doors down from *Manze* is *Sobo* – a stylish café which does a good cappuccino. *Delfina Trust Studios* is at the north end of Bermondsey Street and houses a contemporary art gallery as well as a fine restaurant.

Local Attractions

The only major tourist attraction in the area is the *Imperial War Museum* which is well worth a visit if you have the energy after early morning antique hunting.

Getting a Stall

For further details contact Southwark Council (see appendix).

ABRAHAM ENTERTAINING THE ANGELS.

Bermondsey Market

Borough Market

Southwark Street, SE1

www.boroughmarket.org.uk
Tube: London Bridge (Northern and Jubilee)
Open: Thursday 11am-5pm, Friday 12noon-6pm, Saturday 9am-4pm

It is hard to believe that when the first edition of The London Market Guide was published in 1994, Borough was a wholesale fruit and vegetable market. At that time members of the public were tolerated rather than welcomed as the restaurateurs and caterers went about their business. Since then the market has undergone an incredible transformation becoming one of Europe's leading food markets with thousands of visitors from Thursday to Saturday and many fashionable restaurants, cafés and specialist food outlets, such as *Monmouth Coffee Company* and the *Neal's Yard Dairy,* establishing themselves in the narrow roads around the old market. The transformation began with just a few stalls offering quality food at the weekend. Pioneers, such as the wild boar farmer Peter Gott, struggled as the market found its feet but soon persuaded others to join them as the venture acquired momentum. In the years that followed, the trustees of the market developed and improved the site with the help of architects *Greig + Stephenson* while still preserving the Art Deco exterior on Borough High Street and the 18th century wrought iron structure of the wholesale market. The changes included the expansion of the market into a canopied area between Bedale Street and Southward Cathedral – enabling over 100 additional food stalls to do business here.

Borough has flourished by encouraging all kinds of food retailers and producers to sell at the market and not placed the geographic and production restrictions that are applied at many farmers' markets. The relaxed approach has given rise to a remarkably vibrant food market with all kinds of retailers selling fresh food from around the globe. Here you can find meat sold direct from a single producer such as *Seldom Seen Farm* as well as butchers such as *Ginger Pig,* who sell high quality meat from a number of farms. The cheese stalls are equally varied with Mr Bourne selling his own Cheshire cheese, alongside a specialist parmesan stall and a much larger French delicatessen selling all kinds of cheeses, sausages and other produce. The fruit and vegetables are also exceptional with commercial greengrocers selling produce from around the world alongside specialist stalls including the enterprising French men reviving the tradition of onion selling, including an old bike draped with ropes of succulent pink onions.

At a supermarket you might be lucky to find two or three kinds of mushroom, but at Borough there are over 20 types of fungi available from dried Ceps to the gigantic Puffball. Fishmongers are rarely found at most markets these days, but here there are several elaborate stalls selling anything from shark and conger eel to more familiar staples like cod and salmon. Breads and patisserie are another of Borough's strengths with big names such as *De Gustibus, Konditor & Cook* and *Maison Bertaux* all regulars at the market.

Borough's popularity has enabled specialist food producers to sell profitably to the public in a way that would be impossible anywhere else. One stall specialises in ostrich meat reared on its own farm in England and there are several homemade jam and chutney sellers. The company selling tubs of their own mushroom paté and offering delicious tasters, was so popular that by 3pm they were happily packing up, having sold out. Another Borough success story is *Aunt Alice Puddings*, which sells homemade traditional English puddings to those craving the comfort of nostalgic treats like sticky toffee pudding.

The wine and beer dealers are another important part of the Borough Market's appeal. *Borough Wines* is one of the more established traders, offering all kinds of wines and several fine beers, while *Utobeer* has over 600 different beers from around the world. Other traders just sell their own product such as *New Forest Cider* making its own brand of delicious and unique cider. The one thing all these dealers have in common is the use of small tasters, which is the ideal opportunity to try before you buy.

Borough Market can certainly be an expensive place to shop, but the people that come here love good food and are prepared to pay for it. The atmosphere is infectious with crowds milling from stall to stall, many people sampling the food and chatting with the stallholders. On a recent visit I intended to keep my wallet firmly closed, but returned home laden with French salamis, soft welsh cheese, crusty bread, delicious mushroom paté and spicy chorizo sausage from the Spanish food specialist *Brindisa*. The few bags of shopping may have cost more than at a supermarket but the taste and experience of shopping made it worth the additional expense.

Refreshment

There are numerous places to grab a bite to eat at Borough Market with many stalls cooking take-away food as well as selling produce. One of the fishmongers towards the back of the market sells trays of succulent scallops with lemon while the German bratwurst stall in the canopied area of the market is very popular. In the central market there are a number of butchers that also offer delicious burgers made from their own beef and pork and served with plenty of fresh rocket. *Monmouth Coffee Company* is a great place to get a strong cappuccino while *Maria's Café* offers great value traditional caff food for those on a tight budget.

Getting a Stall

Contact Borough Market on 020 7407 1002 or visit their website (boroughmarket.org.uk) to enquire about renting a stall at either the wholesale or retail market.

Borough Market

Choumert Road

a   Choumert Road
b   Rye Lane

Rye Lane end of Choumert Rd, and Atwell Rd opposite, SE15

Rail: Peckham Rye (London Bridge)
Open: Monday-Saturday 9.30am-5pm

One of London's Chartered Markets, Choumert Road has been here for well over a hundred years. Many of the fifteen or so stalls that set up here are old, wooden carts which have been wheeled around the market for so many years that the wooden wheels are almost worn to the axle. The old stalls have seen a lot of changes in the market as well as in the make-up of the local community. The influx of international food shops has brought competition to Choumert Road, but the market looks as though it has enough scruffy charisma to keep going – at least until the wheels finally fall off the wagon.

The stalls (pitched close to the row of specialist food shops to create a colourful corridor of produce) still attract a steady flow of customers with plenty of bargains and friendly banter. Whether you're cooking Moroccan, Thai or Afro-Caribbean, one of Choumert Road's traders should be able to supply the ingredients.

Local rivalry keeps the prices pretty cheap, with lots of special discounts for those buying in larger quantities. Across Rye Lane at the end of Atwell Street there is an additional fruit and veg stall which has the locals queuing up, so shop around.

Getting a Stall

For further details contact Southwark Council (see Appendix)

Rye Lane

48 Rye Lane, between ElmGrove
and High Shore Road, SE15

Rail: Peckham Rye
Open: Monday-Saturday 9.30am-6.30pm, Sunday 11am-5pm

In 2000 the market shut for a major refurbishment. The new market is a much more attractive place to shop. The entrance has kept the same Art Deco design but in place of peeling plaster and a tatty sign, is a clean white exterior with a stylish steel arch. Inside, the improvement is even more evident with a glass roofed passageway leading to a main hall with about 50 clean, new units. The central part of this L shaped market is still a little dark, but the painted floors and bright lighting have banished the grim and rather damp atmosphere of the old market.

It would be good if the stall-holders within the market had sharpened up their act to match the new environment, but the traders have not changed much and the new building is quiet even on a Friday afternoon when Rye Lane is busy. Among the things on offer are mobile phone accessories, a selection of household goods and toiletries, carpets, pet food and accessories, a black music stall, shoes, street fashion and African foodstuffs. Despite the refurbishment the main problem with this market is the lack of good food stalls which would encourage people to visit the market as part of their weekly shop.

Refreshment

Le Petit Jardin Café is a pleasant if inappropriately named café in the middle of the market which serves a good cappuccino.

Getting a Stall

For further details contact the market office on 020 7732 2202.

Deptford Market

Deptford Market

Deptford High Street, SE8
(Deptford Broadway to Deptford Station)
Rail: Deptford
Open: Wednesday, Friday and Saturday 8.30am-5pm

Although Deptford is just a fifteen minute bus ride from Greenwich, it has none of its famous neighbour's tourist attractions and Deptford Market is largely unknown outside the area. The market itself is huge, extending over half the length of Deptford High Street and also along Douglas Way – including a large flea market in Douglas Square on Wednesdays and Saturdays. The combination of a lively street market, along with a cheap junk market, is a good one. A visitor to Deptford on a Saturday can do all the weekly essential shopping, but also indulge in the hunt for inexpensive bric-à-brac. Markets that offer this kind of interesting shopping are rare these days and Deptford is beginning to stand out as one of the best such markets to visit on a Saturday. One of the most interesting things to happen in Deptford recently has been the arrival of an old railway carriage – deposited in a courtyard, just opposite Griffin Street, and converted into a trendy café. There are even ambitious plans to have a crafts, arts and food market in the courtyard surrounding the café on Saturdays and Sundays.

Deptford Church Street and Douglas Way

The main thoroughfares of the market have over 150 stalls offering a great selection of basics like fresh fruit and veg, fresh fish, street fashion, bags and shoes, toiletries and household goods, perfume, watches, pet food and accessories. The market also has some outstanding specialist stalls dealing in car accessories, household blinds and a very well-stocked stall offering cheap brand name hairdryers and hair clippers. The top end of the market even has a trader selling beds, with a choice of eight styles standing on the pavement. Although many markets have stalls selling pots and pans, Deptford has just about the largest cooking pot known to man for a mere £60. Cooking pans large enough to feed an army are not going to be of general interest, but it is an indication of the range of wares to be found at the market. Food is not one of the market's strong points, but there are enough good fruit and veg stalls to allow visitors to stock up on good value produce although the range is limited. The fresh fish stall is the most interesting food stall on the market with plenty of scaly things from which to choose and the novelty of large cat fish swimming around in a shallow tank awaiting their fate. Some of the best value clothing stalls are on Douglas Way with one trader offering colourful summer dresses for just £5 and another selling name-less jeans for just £12.

Douglas Square Flea Market

Every Wednesday and Saturday Douglas Square is filled with about 40 stalls offering a sprawling assortment of bric-à-brac, used clothing, electrical goods, DVDs, jewellery and furniture. No attempt to display the goods is really made with clothes piled high on tables and boxes of assorted items just put on the floor. Piles of books are stacked on stalls and pavement and sold for as just 50p each and there are many larger items like lawn mowers and hi-fis sold for just a fiver but without any guarantee except the word of the trader. The clothing is sold in a similarly chaotic manner with mountains of garments to sift through and most sold for just £1. Amid all the dross there are plenty of bargains to be unearthed such as the fine cotton shirt discovered here for just 50p. Many of London's best flea markets have now closed which makes Douglas Square a rare gem in the shopping landscape of London. The flea market starts and finishes earlier than the rest of Deptford Market, even on fine summer days traders start packing up by 2.30 in the afternoon.

Refreshment

There are several good places to enjoy a meal around the market with the arrival of the *Deptford Project Café* offering the novelty of enjoying a cappuccino in an old railway carriage. *The Bear Café* is a good place to get a drink and something to eat and lies north of the market just beyond the railway bridge. If you fancy a taste of something a little more traditional there are two pie and mash shops just a little further north. .

Local Attractions

There are numerous decent food shops along Deptford High Street that add to the market's appeal, including several good butchers, fishmongers and one specialising in farm fresh eggs. If the flea market hasn't exhausted your thirst for second-hand goods there are several excellent charity shops along the High Street and a very good retro clothing shop called *Rag 'n' Bones* at no.40 Deptford High Street. If you enjoy church architecture take a look at St Paul's Church, just north of the market – a wonderful example of a baroque church which lies in pleasant grounds..

Getting a Stall

For further details contact Lewisham Council (see Appendix)

East Street

East Street

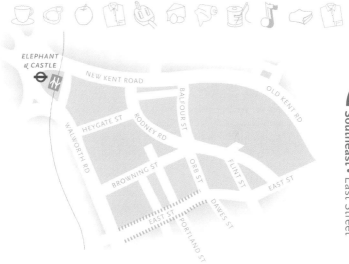

East Street between Walworth Road and Dawes Street, SE17

Tube: Elephant & Castle (Northern, Bakerloo
Open: Tuesday-Sunday 8.30am-4pm (busiest at weekends, when the street's shops are open both days)

The birthplace of Charlie Chaplin, East Street is also home to one of South London's biggest, busiest and loudest markets. At weekends, with stalls squeezed between shops along the length of this long street, it begins to look like Oxford Street in miniature – tides of determined shoppers weave around clumps of slow-moving bargain hunters as the queues build for cut-price essentials. Surrounded by some of the area's largest housing estates, East Street has a long history of serving the practical needs of local people, so craft fair trinkets are nowhere to be seen on stalls crammed with all things useful, wearable or edible.

Unlike a lot of other markets, in East Street you can still find a genuine sense of community, with lots of classic South London humour, a real mix of shoppers, plenty of banter and noisily competitive traders stoking the lively atmosphere. The market isn't a wise choice for the delicate or the hung over, with lots of noise and bustle as thousands of people make their way between the stalls. On busy days you will need to watch out for serious jostlers, and East Street can also bring new meaning to the phrase "price wars" as you get caught in the crossfire between sellers as phrases like "Oi! Come on, who wants a bargain?", "Two pounds of mush' a nicker" are bellowed for all to hear. But the demonstrations of iron-larynxed stamina and word-mangling delivery make brilliant free entertainment. My favourite is the burly fruit and veg man at the far end of the market who makes good comic use of his incongruously high-pitched voice to draw in the punters.

The size of the market means that rival traders have to compete on price, so make sure you don't part with your cash without first checking out the opposition. East Street is surprisingly long and from its start on Walworth Road it's quite a trek to the far end, at the junction with Dawes Street. The market offers all the staples, with lots of great bargains for the discerning shopper amongst piles of household and electrical goods, CDs, bedding and carpets, sweets, luggage, perfume, toiletries, jewellery, toys, fruit and veg (some Caribbean as well as standard English), wholesale meat, plants and flowers. The local Chinese community are also beginning to make their presence felt on the market with some very fine Oriental handbags for only £7 and another stall offering Chinese medicine with things like tea that claims to help discourage smoking.

Certain things do stand out. East Street is full of clothes, and many of the shops and stalls offer impressive reductions on chain store prices – underwear, dresses, and shirts are often good value – although sifting is essential as much of the stock is definitely more cheap than chic. A number of haberdashery and material stalls – as well as the excellent Barney's Textile Centre – also offer D.I.Y. fashion bunnies the chance to create some pretty snazzy outfits. One of the longest running haberdashers is run by an elderly and almost deaf trader who makes a great display of his wares from his ancient wooden stall and offers most items for between 50p and £1. The shoe stalls also carry a wide range with some persuasive prices, like the one selling piles of women's leather sandals for just £4 a pair. There are a few good stalls offering cut flowers and plants throughout the week, but on Sundays Blackwood Street becomes a dedicated area for flowers and plants with about six large stalls showing up here. The choice is very good and there are plenty of bargains with large trays of Busy Lizzies for just £4 and plenty of healthy looking shrubs for around a fiver.

East Street

Refreshment

Once you've battled through the bargains, East Street isn't short of culinary pit stops. Right along its length, the market is dotted with pubs, stalls and cafés. Local favourites include the *Market Grill*, *Starlite Café*, *Jack's Café* and the *Golden Café* all of which offer good basic grub. For food on the go there is the long established *East Street Burger Stand*, located towards the far end of the market.

Local Attractions

There is not much to attract visitors to this part of town, but on a Sunday Westmoreland Road Market is well worth a visit if you like sifting through junk for bargains (see page 162).

Getting a Stall

For further details contact Southwark Council (see appendix).

Elephant & Castle

Outside Elephant & Castle shopping centre ,SE1

Tube: Elephant & Castle (Northern and Bakerloo)
Rail: Elephant & Castle (Blackfriars)
Open: Monday-Saturday 9.30am-5pm

This market circles the famous Elephant and Castle shopping centre at below ground level and has been trading for about ten years. Unfortunately, its location – stuck under the centre's concrete petticoats with the smell of the municipal toilet never far away – hasn't helped to establish much of an atmosphere. People surfacing from the labyrinthine tunnels under the Elephant's twin roundabouts seem mainly concentrated on their journey, so you don't feel very encouraged to potter. The selection of goods on offer is pretty uninspiring, focusing on new clothes, sportswear, accessories, jewellery, watches, toys, electrical and household goods and toiletries, but you might uncover the odd genuine bargain if you persevere. One such find was the stall selling a reasonably good choice of sunglasses for £4 each.

On the sartorial front, some stalls stock slightly more interesting and fashionable women's clothes, but the emphasis is on cheap, functional separates aimed generally at a more middle-aged customer. A few traders have £1 rails or jumble-style trestles with mixes of second-hand clothes, but there are few choice items in amongst the nylon nasties of yesteryear. The large shoe stall had some reasonable deals, with some interesting brand name trainers for around £25.

Elephant & Castle

Refreshment
As well as the Latin food outlets in the shopping centre the market also has a good selection of lively food stalls, selling either Thai, Caribbean or African snacks.

Local Attractions
Although the market isn't worth a special visit, if you do happen to pass through and have time to kill, take a quick look in the shopping centre itself. It may be a much-maligned example of soulless retail architecture, but the Elephant's infamous centrepiece hides a few things that counter the general tone of strip-lit blandness. Opposite *Woolworth's*, *Tlon Books* stocks a surprisingly comprehensive selection of competitively priced second-hand fiction and non-fiction titles. The first floor of the centre has become a meeting place for Peckham's Latin American community with a great Latin Music outlet and several places to get authentic South American food and coffee.

Getting a Stall
For further details about getting a stall phone 020 7708 2313.

Greenwich Market

a) Greenwich Market
b) The Village Market   THAMES
c) Clock Tower Market

Greenwich Church Street, Stockwell Street, Greenwich High Road, SE10

DLR: Cutty Sark
Rail: Greenwich (London Bridge)
River Boat: This is a great way to see the Thames and visit the market. There are riverboats running from Westminster, Embankment and Tower pier every Sunday to Greenwich. For details contact Greenwich Tourist Office on 020 8858 6376
Open: Saturday and Sunday 9.30am-5pm (all parts of the market)
Wednesday 9.30am-5pm (food court at the main market)
Thursday 9.30am-5pm (collectables market within the main market)
Friday 9am-5pm (crafts market within the main market)

Greenwich has a fantastic market and in recent years it seems to have improved after a slight dip in fortunes in the late 90's. Like other major markets such as Camden and Portobello, there is not one market but several offering different things and open at varying times. Greenwich is different from the other two large markets because of its maritime history and location on the Thames, offering spectacular views of the City (best enjoyed from the top of Greenwich Park). The Thames is ever present here and gives the place a seaside atmosphere – particularly on fine days when it is like a cross between Portobello Market and Brighton seafront. If you visit on a Thursday or Friday only the main covered market will be open, and Greenwich will seem rather quiet and restful. On Sundays Greenwich is at its busiest. If you don't like crowds and the hustle and bustle of a busy market, Saturday is the best day to visit.

Greenwich Market

Entrances on Greenwich Church Street, College Approach,
King William Walk and Nelson Road
www.greenwichmarket.net
Open: Wednesday 11am-7pm, Thursday-Friday 10am-5pm (arts & crafts,
antiques and collectables),
Saturday-Sunday 10am-5.30pm (arts and crafts and Food Court)
This part of Greenwich is the oldest surviving market having acquired a royal charter in 1700 – although in those days it traded wholesale in fruit and veg rather than the arts, crafts, collectables and fine food that are sold here today. The buildings around the courtyard have not changed and the cobbled stones and paving are still original, but a modern roof has been added in the last 25 years which lets in natural light while keeping out the elements.

In recent years the fresh food part of the market has really taken off and these days about a quarter of the market area is a dedicated food area with lots of food to eat as you shop and plenty to take away and be enjoyed at home. Among the interesting stalls is a large and well stocked Italian deli with all kinds of cheese and prepared meats as well as more unusual things like authentic Italian nougat cake. There are several excellent bread and patisserie stalls offering a bewildering choice of yeasty treats and several stalls offering the fresh salads and olives to make a meal of it. The sausage stall is a firm favourite with a choice of traditional bangers from pork and leek to spicy chilli pork, as well as a variety of salamis. In terms of food to eat as you go the Turkish stall was one of my favourites with a host of mezze and wraps to try and lots of sweet Turkish pastries. The tapas stall is also popular, as is *Newberry's Oyster Bar* who offer a quick taste of the sea for £1 a shot. The food area has proved a great success and the opening hours have now been extended to include Wednesdays.

The rest of the market is largely dedicated to new designer and craft goods with more of an emphasis on vintage and collectables on a Thursday. At the weekend you will have plenty of good quality gear to choose from among the 50 or so stalls, including several independent fashion labels such as *Nebali* that sell their stylish dresses here for £45. *Jones* handmade clothing is also a regular at the weekends, offering bargains like rain coats for £30 and summer dresses for £35. If you are looking for a new bag then this market is definitely a good place to look with one dealer selling colourful imported bags from Hong Kong for around £30 while there are several independent designers such as *Dolly Apples* who offers her own handmade bags for as little as £15 and wonderful skirts, made from vintage fabrics, for £48. Complimenting the fashion designers there is lots of jewellery, from funky plastic jewellery designed for the teenage market to more pricey individually designed silverware. Other dealers offered a wide selection of gifts including framed art work and photos, scented soaps, funky T-shirts and one unusual stall selling kitchen utensils made from olive tree wood with bargains such as a pestle and mortar for a reasonable £18. There are quite a few stalls catering for babies and kids with *Bea's Beastlies* (www.beasbeastlies.co.uk) attracting a small crowd of young enthusiasts for her warped, but still cute, soft toys.

The antiques and collectables market held here on a Thursday is ideal if you want to avoid the Sunday crowds. About forty stalls set up here selling all kinds of things such as cheap paperbacks, classical CDs from £4, interesting old toys and collectables – from 70s kitsch articles to Russian oil paintings from the 30s. Compared to the weekends, the market is very quiet with stall-holders reading the papers or chatting with an occasional customer and plenty of room in the local eateries to relax and inspect your purchases.

Refreshment

One of the best things about this market is its relaxed atmosphere and numerous eating and drinking venues. Among the places to sit and relax with a pint are *The Coach and Horses* and *Admiral Hardy* pubs, or try the *George II Café* housed within the market. The food court has lots of stalls offering delicious food if you don't mind eating on the move.

Getting a Stall

For further details contact the market office on 020 8293 3110, or try the company's head office on 020 7515 7153.

Greenwich Market

The Village Market

Stockwell Street
Open: Saturday-Sunday 9am-5pm

This part of Greenwich has not changed very much in the last ten years and is still a mix of stalls, lock up units made from metal containers and a ramshackle indoor area at the back. This kind of low budget sprawling market is rare in the capital these days and this makes the Village more of a charming oddity. It is certainly one of the best markets for an eclectic mix of furniture, new and second-hand clothing, bric-à-brac, collectable vinyl, CDs and books. There are lots dealers specialising in quality vintage clothes including the permanent shop called 360 Degrees Vintage. The indoor furniture centre offers a mix of new reproduction furniture along with a few genuine antiques.

Sadly this unusual and rare market is due to be demolished to make way for another unoriginal complex of shops and flats, with only 11 pitches allocated for the continuation of the market. The market will continue for a little longer, but building will begin in 2010 when this wonderful part of Greenwich will disappear.

Clock Tower Market

Clock Tower Market

Greenwich High Road (next to the Greenwich Cinema)
Open: Saturday and Sunday 9am-5pm

On a busy Sunday about fifty stalls set-up next to *Greenwich Cinema*, although there are fewer on a Saturday and, being open air, this market is vulnerable to the weather. On a good day you can find retro clothes, fine new and antique bed linen, antique cutlery, some interesting pieces of furniture, books, a stall specialising in framed mirrors, and several dealers in old postcards, coins and other collectables. One stallholder had an unusual stock of antiques and collectables imported from France including a few stuffed animals and a large floral ceiling light – a bargain at just £65. One of the best aspects of this market is the selection of collectable and costume jewellery at reasonable prices, including a fine vintage amber bracelet for only £24. One regular trader sells oil paintings with all the charm of a West End art dealer and stocks anything from a small watercolours for £5 to a large contemporary oil painting for £800. The CD stall shows equal discrimination in its selection of stock with an emphasis on Jazz, Gospel and Classical music. This is one of the best parts of Greenwich, but is a little off the main path followed by visitors and, for this reason, traders are often willing to barter and there are always one or two stalls selling items to clear. An example of this was the elderly Russian gentleman who was trying to get rid of a set of elaborate painted wall and ceiling lights which were originally £85, but were on sale for only £20. This small courtyard is one of the few specialist antiques and collectables markets remaining in London and one of the best.

Refreshment

Next door to the market is a modern pub which is not particularly charming, but does have the advantage of outside seating on fine days. .

Getting a Stall

For further details about trading at the market phone Jane on 020 7237 2001.

Lewisham High Street

North end of Lewisham High Street, SE13

Rail: Lewisham or Ladywell (Charing Cross, Waterloo & London Bridge)
Open: Monday-Saturday 9am-5pm

Hemmed in by chain stores and flanking the Lewisham Centre, this functional market nonetheless appears to be holding its own. Even on a weekday, a steady flow of shoppers cruise the line of stalls stocking up on standard market fare. Although unremarkable, the market's jaunty, bulb-lit stalls and friendly atmosphere make it a fun place to buy groceries: the fruit and veg stalls offer a wide selection, with other stalls selling flowers, fish, eggs, new clothes, watches, household goods, cheap ornaments, underwear, cards, make-up and haberdashery. The fish stall is a particular favourite with its impressive display of everyday fish along with more unusual things like octopus and eel.

Refreshment

Lewisham High Street has several caffs serving standard British food, the most popular being *Something Fishy*.

Getting a Stall

For further details contact Lewisham Council (see appendix).

North Cross Road

North Cross Rd (from Lordship Lane to Fellbrigg Rd), SE22

Rail: East Dulwich
Open: Saturdays 10am-5pm

There have been a few sad tales of decline among London's markets since the last edition of this book, but there have also been a few success stories. In the last five years this market has grown from just a couple of stalls to about twenty, offering a great mix of quality food, vintage and new clothing, bric-à-brac, furniture, jewellery, CDs, books and even original photography.

One of the reasons for the market's recent success appears to be the growing prosperity of the area with lots of smart shops, cafés and well maintained Victorian terraced housing. Just like Northcote Road (see page 122) this market thrives because it appeals to the well-heeled middle-classes who are looking for a shopping experience and not so concerned about finding the lowest price, unlike the traditional weekday markets that have lost business to the supermarkets.

North Cross Road begins with the longest serving trader at the market. Jeff Bowman has been selling fresh fish here from Thursday to Saturday for the last 25 years and is pleased to see the market taking off. Another market favourite is *G.G. Sparkes Organic Butchers* which always has a queue of people on Saturdays prepared to pay a little extra for better quality organic produce. These traders are complimented by a salami stall, a good quality bakers and a popular salad bar. The market could benefit from a fruit and veg stall, but there is a smart greengrocers and deli shop about half way along the road which provides the locals with fresh, seasonal produce.

Northcote Road

One of the best things about this market is the range of vintage clothing and household goods available. One offered a mixture of stylish 60s items from ashtrays to larger things like tables and chairs. As well as the household goods there were also a few items of clothing from that era complimented by the new clothing stall opposite which sells colourful tops for £5-10 and full dresses for £25. Another stall specialises in vintage and reproduction mirrors with lots of styles and all of the stock carefully displayed to allow shoppers to inspect the stock and themselves at the same time. Lovers of all things vintage and retro should not miss the vintage store at the top of the market, just off Fellbrigg Road. This shop is open throughout the week, but on Saturdays displays a selection of clothing, furniture, books and bric-à-brac from tables outside.

Other interesting stalls on the market include the bookseller offering a selection of paperbacks and the CD dealer, who has a great choice of World Music and Modern Jazz and has acquired a loyal following among the local music buffs. There are several good jewellery stalls offering both vintage and original designs, as well as traders selling colourful woven bags and baskets and well-made linen clothing. The same ladies that sell stylish women's gear on Northcote Road also have a stall at the top end of this market close to Tim Coutts who displays some of his contemporary furniture here every Saturday. Neil Williams has one of the last stalls, where he displays a selection of his very fine landscapes of London which range in price from £60 to £300.

North Cross Road is certainly not the most practical market in terms of doing a weekly shop but it is a fun place to spend a few hours and there are enough appealing things here to insure that most visitors will not leave empty handed.

Refreshment
There are two excellent Cafés on North Cross Road – *Blue Mountain Café* and *The Drum*.

Local Attractions
The Dulwich Picture Gallery and *The Horniman Museum* are both in the area and excellent places to enjoy some culture after a hard mornings shopping.

Getting a Stall
For further details contact Southwark Council (see appendix).

Southwark Park Road

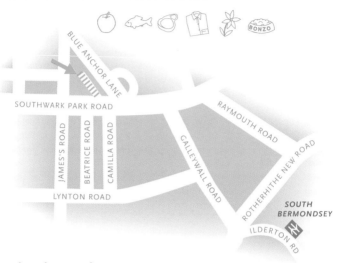

(The Blue Market)
Market Place off Southwark Park Road, SE16

Rail: South Bermondsey
Open: Monday-Saturday 9.30am-5pm

Poor old Southwark Park Road. Stuck well below the Thames, lined with squat sixties shoe-box shop units and sandwiched between squalid estates and railway lines, the location doesn't exactly scream hotspot. In the seventies the council made things worse by giving the road over entirely to the relentless south-eastwards bound traffic, side-lining its once-famous street market into a bland precinct. Even now, despite the pretty ash trees and bright municipal benches, the market's slightly artificial setting doesn't seem to help pull in passing trade from the busy High Street. The Sainsburys at Surrey Quays is also leeching the market's customers. The council have attempted to re-brand the market, calling it "The Blue Market" and erecting a sign to advertise the fact. The name derives from Blue Anchor Lane, which is just around the corner.

But it's not all gloom and doom. Although in terms of its range of goods the market isn't exceptional, there is still a bit of atmosphere about the place and most traders seem to welcome banter with regulars. On offer is the usual mixture of things decorative, edible or wearable (Saturdays bring out the most stalls): cheap men's clothes, sports gear, shoes and trainers, nightwear and undies, as well as an excellent pet stall. But, as a local market, Southwark Park Road plays to its strengths, the best stalls being those piled high with cheaply priced fruit, veg, eggs, fish, seafood and flowers.

The friendly fruit and veg man has plenty of regulars popping by for a pound of this or that, and with good reason. Although unremarkable in terms of the trendy or exotic, his produce includes some unusual indigenous varieties of fruit. The plant and flower stall is also excellent, with healthy bedding plants and an impressive selection of bulbs.

Local Attractions
There is a good butchers in Market Place which complements the food offered at the stalls, and also a reasonable *Sue Ryder* shop for those interested in second-hand goods. One of the best charity shops in London is to be found just behind *The Blue Anchor*. It is a courtyard rather than a shop, and is crammed full of interesting second-hand clubber.

Refreshment
If you're looking for somewhere to eat the *Pop-In Café* just opposite the market does no-frills British grub. *The Blue Anchor* is one of the street's landmarks and serves a good pint.

Getting a Stall
For further details contact Southwark Council (see appendix)

Westmoreland Road

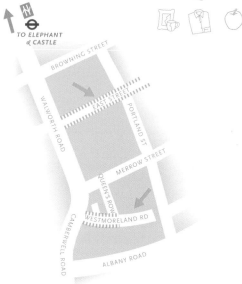

TO ELEPHANT & CASTLE

Westmoreland Street, off the Walworth Road, SE17

Tube: Elephant & Castle (Northern, Bakerloo)
Open: Sundays 8am-1pm (bric-à-brac)

Westmoreland Road weekday market has always struggled in the shadow of the fabulous East Street Market, just five minutes walk north along the Walworth Road. The weekday market has now dwindled to just one solitary fruit and veg stall while East Street is still a thriving place. Things are different on Sundays when Westmoreland really comes into its own as a flea market with about forty stalls displaying their tatty wears along the entire length of the road. On Sunday mornings the market is buzzing with a chatty mixture of locals from the surrounding estates and visitors from further afield, all on the lookout for a serious bargain. And there are plenty to be had amongst the tidal wave of clobber and clothes, much of which is just dumped in piles on the pavement, or spills out of vans, old prams or boxes. The shambolic presentation means prices are very low, so there are plenty of 50p wonders to be had if you are prepared to get stuck in.

A lot of the stuff on offer is sub-jumble junk, with broken and dirty casualties from decades past lined up with larger items like fridges, stereos and furniture, but a few stall-holders seem to have weeded out the rubbish and stock attractive and unusual retro knick-knacks and ephemera like cocktail glasses, jewellery, clocks and picture frames – mostly going for less than a fiver. As with any junk market, shoppers are often sifting through the detritus of other people's lives and this was very evident at one stall where a large box of family memorabilia including some photo albums and a collection of letters could be picked-up for just a fiver. A fascinating, if rather sad, bargain.

Household items such as old cutlery, pans and crockery are also worth a look, as are the numerous boxes of books to be found on many of the stalls – amongst the dentist's surgery-style reads are a few more recent titles going for next to nothing. There used to be some new clothing stalls at the Sunday market, but the clothes are now all second-hand with rails of 50p and £1 items everywhere. Although some stalls may throw up the odd find, this is not likely to be the best hunting ground for retro purists. Music, though, is everywhere, with CDs, records and tape stocks on many of the stalls. Those who enjoy looking through boxes of old vinyl for the occasional gem will not be disappointed. Among the recent bargains found here was an old hand whisk in perfect condition for just £2 and a large bag of plastic kids toys which had plenty of trinkets and things to keep the kids quiet for just 50p. Westmoreland Road may be a bit on the rough side, but that is part of the market's appeal. Cheap flea market dealers can only make a living selling in cheap and fairly down-at-heel markets, so if you want the quirky bargains you may have to explore parts of London that are off the tourist map.

Refreshment

The only place to eat on the street is the *Café Silam* which is OK for basic grub. For some really good food try the award winning *La Luna Pizzeria*, which is on Walworth Road, just opposite the market.

Local Attractions

The biggest attraction in this part of town is East Street Market, just a few minutes walk north (see page 145 for further details). On Sundays Blackwood Street, just off East Street, is dedicated to flowers and plants and is a great place to pick-up some flora for the garden after sifting through the bric-à-brac of Westmoreland Road.

Getting a Stall

For further details contact Southwark Council (see appendix).

Westmoreland Road

Woolwich

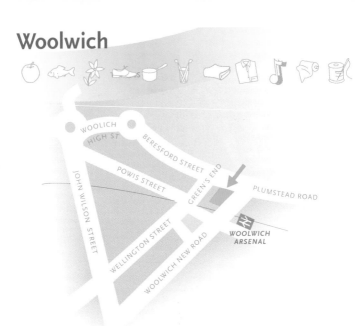

Rail: Woolwich Arsenal (London Bridge); (or take the ferry south across the Thames from Woolwich North (North London Line)).
Open: Tuesday, Wednesday, Friday and Saturday 8.30am-5pm, Thursday 8.30am-2pm

Downstream from the Thames Barrier and easily eclipsed by the more glamorous and intact attractions of nearby Greenwich, Woolwich feels like a place nudged just outside the radar of central London's interest. Historically, Woolwich played an essential role in the Capital's economy as the home of both the Royal Dockyard and Royal Arsenal, but those industries have long gone and it seems resigned to being just another slice of inner suburbia.

Woolwich Market (setting up under the Arsenal Gate in Beresford Square since well before the turn of the century), does something to break up the slightly anonymous town centre with a lively range of functional and frivolous goods aimed mainly at the local population. Essentially operating as a standard provisions market with a contingent of clothes stalls, Woolwich holds few surprises and as such is probably not worth a lengthy trip.

That said, if you live locally or just happen to be in the area, the market does offer excellent fruit and vegetables. As you enter the market from the Woolwich New Road, an impressive spread of traditional greens and predominantly British fruits opens out along a triangle of stalls – load up on everything for a stew or salad for just a few pounds. The remainder of the square's stalls are made up of street market standards, household goods and toiletries, shoes, cheap clothes, carpets, toys and computer games, children's clothes, brand-a-like sportswear, football kits, pet food, hair accessories and jewellery, bags and luggage, bedding and underwear. Woolwich has great flowers, with a number of stalls offering very tempting prices on both traditional and more exotic blooms and the material and haberdashery traders are also great value.

Refreshment

There are a number of friendly greasy spoon cafés round the perimeter of the market, but if you fancy something a bit more substantial, *Kenroy's Pie & Eel Shop* is on Woolwich New Road.

Getting a Stall

For further details about a stall at either Woolwich Market contact Greenwich Council (see appendix).

East

Bethnal Green Road

Bethnal Green Road (Vallance Road to Wilmot Street), E2
Tube: Bethnal Green (Central Line)
Open: Monday-Saturday 8.30am-5pm, Thursday 8.30am-12.30pm

There has been a market on Bethnal Green Road since the 19th century, and despite the arrival of a Tesco store and the neglect of the local council, Bethnal Green Market is still going strong. The market is an expression of the East End's continued vitality and on any weekday you will see old East Enders rubbing shoulders with Asian and African locals, as well as more recent arrivals from Eastern Europe. Despite the mix of people and cultures, the atmosphere is friendly with plenty of banter and many traders taking the chance for a chat with regulars when things are a little quiet. This must be one of the reasons for the longevity of the market with people preferring to shop on the street with people they know, than to endure the anonymous experience of supermarket shopping.

As a fairly large, well-established market with a solid base of local customers and a string of competing traders, Bethnal Green Road provides a wide range of goods at persuasive prices. Everything you might need, from bedding to plugs, is available and generally of reliable quality. There is nothing particularly out of the ordinary here, but if you're after a relaxed, no frills, market then this one should fit the bill.

The fruit and vegetables are cheap and fresh, but at this market mangetout is given the cold shoulder in favour of less exotic fare such as broad beans. One stall compensated for its lack of foreign veg with six different types of potato – a range that would put most stalls on Berwick Street Market to shame. The exception to this rule is the Asian fruit and veg stall which has a bewildering display of bitter gourd, fenugreek and jackfruit and is popular with the local Asian community. A few of the street's shops also sell food from period piece premises – evidence that this area seems to have avoided the total destruction of its retail traditions by the convenience revolution.

Bethnal Green has a reasonable selection of clothes stalls, with a spectrum of new men's and women's clothing ranging from middle-aged and functional to semi-designer jeans and jackets. Prices are often, to quote one trader's sign, 'Bloody Cheap!', and there are indeed plenty of solid bargains on standard items like sweat tops, leggings and T-shirts. One dealer was doing well with his end-of-season ladies fashion from high street names like *Principles* and *M&S*, with many garments sold for a fiver. A number of rummage-style stalls also have super cheap separates or a lucky dip mixture of things like lipsticks, suntan lotion and hair products. The luggage and bags sold on the market are also slightly better looking than the drably functional clobber you get elsewhere. One of the longest established traders on the market offers a vast selection of toiletries and kitchen cleaning materials at very low prices. The stallholder explained that her grandfather had run a stall on the same site in the 40s and 50s and although the gene had skipped a generation she was happy to be continuing the family tradition.

The market has shrunk a little since the last the last edition of the book and during the week one old fruit and veg stall stands alone at the Vallance Road end of the market. The council want Norman and his stall to move into the main body of the market to make way for parking meters, but he has been trading on the site for nearly 25 years and isn't going to move. Good luck Norman!

Refreshment

There are lots of snack bars and cafés along the course of Bethnal Green Market. *G.Kelly* serves pie and mash in a textbook marble and benches interior, while *E.Pellici* does Italian-cum-greasy spoon breakfasts and lunches. The latter has 'local institution' written all over it: on site since 1900, this tiny café has beautiful Art Deco woodwork, yellowing celebrity photos, genuinely charming staff, good quality comfort food and bags of collective charisma.

Local Attractions

The main attraction in this part of town is *The Museum of Childhood* which is at the eastern end of Bethnal Green Road, on Cambridge Heath Road and is a great place to take children of all ages. Another interesting destination is the newly developed *Oxford House* which has two art galleries and a café, as well as daily fitness classes and is just behind the market on Derbyshire Street.

Getting a Stall

For further details contact Tower Hamlets Central Market Office (see appendix).

Bethnal Green Road

Billingsgate

North quay of West India Dock, Isle of Dogs, E14
DLR: West India Quay
Open: Tuesday-Saturday 5am-8.30am

Billingsgate fish market moved to this modern warehouse in January 1982 from its City location in Lower Thames Street, where it had been trading for nearly a thousand years. Billingsgate's new premises lack the grandeur of the old building (which was designed by Sir Horace Jones) but, given the commercial nature of the market and the volume of traffic in the City, such a pragmatic move was inevitable. The new market, although ugly from the outside, still has a great atmosphere and continues the great tradition of London's fish trade.

A stone's throw away from Canary Wharf, the market is easy to find – one dead giveaway are the seagulls which constantly circle above it, some of whom have grown huge on the fishy titbits so readily in supply here. The place is busiest between 6.30am and 8am when most of the commercial buyers are doing business – haggling over prices and checking the quality of the stock. Some of the traders are wholesale only, but it's worth asking as many will sell to individual customers and newcomers are always given a friendly welcome. It's a great place to come with a recipe in mind and hunt down the freshest ingredients possible – just watch out for the forklift trucks operating at the entrance to the market. Among the fifty or so traders you can find every kind of fish imaginable, such as white sturgeon, spotted dogfish and large catfish still wriggling around in their polystyrene boxes. There's also a comprehensive selection of crustaceans and molluscs with anything from deep-water shrimps to live lobsters with their pincers bound to prevent an unwelcome nip.

Refreshment
There are two cafés on the premises but they cater largely for the porters and, although you will be made to feel welcome, you will have to tolerate the ever-present aroma of fish.

Brick Lane

a) Backyard Market
b) Sunday Upmarket

Brick Lane (north of the railway bridge up to Bethnal Green Road), Bethnal Green Road (from Brick Lane to Commercial Street), Cheshire and Sclater Street, E1-E2
Tube: Liverpool Street (Metro & Circle Lines), Aldgate East (District), Old Street (Northern), Shoreditch High Street (East London Line – open 2010)
Open: Sunday 6am-1pm (Street Market),
Sunday 10am-5pm (The Backyard Market and Upmarket)
Saturday 10am-5pm (The Backyard Market)

With so many of London's markets being ordered to conform with local government regulations Brick Lane is a last bastion of disorder and lawlessness and is all the better for that. Building work for the East London line extension has closed many of the railway arches that were once a feature of the market, but the hundreds of fly pitchers that show up here every Sunday always find a new area of pavement to display their wares. Many of these itinerant traders that sell junk from a blanket have simply decamped onto the central part of Brick Lane, but on a recent visit building work had forced them to move again onto the far end of Cheshire Street and no doubt they are destined to move again in the coming months. This Hydra-like quality of Brick Lane is infuriating for those trying to write about it but makes the shopping experience a lot more fun – keep your eyes peeled for new streets that have succumbed to market fever.

The area has also been transformed by the arrival of two new markets – the Sunday Upmarket and Backyard Market. These two large industrial and parking areas have been adapted into market spaces on a Sunday and have proved such a success that the Backyard Market is now the first in the area to start trading on a Saturday. These new arrivals have succeeded by providing a place where East London's small businesses and designers can sell direct to the public and provide the quality arts and crafts that Brick Lane lacked until their arrival. The different parts of the market are dealt with separately below, but expect changes as this part of town is still in a state of flux.

Bethnal Green Road
(from Sclater Street to Commercial Street)

Wheeler Street and the archways disappeared over 5 years ago to make way for the new East London Line which is still under construction. Huge cranes loom over Bethnal Green Road, but the itinerant traders are not easily discouraged and many of them moved onto Bethnal Green Road taking with them their odd assortment of second-hand clothes, bric-à-brac, books, CDs and vinyl, cameras and bikes. The chaotic squalor of this part of the market will horrify some visitors, but for hardcore bargain hunters it is heaven. The long-term effect of the new tube line is difficult to predict but whatever changes there are, this spontaneous part of the market seems destined to continue in one way or another.

Brick Lane, Cheshire Street

The Sunday Upmarket

Brick Lane

Brick Lane, Cheshire Street

The Backyard Market

Brick Lane, Cheshire Street

Sclater Street

The junction with Bethnal Green Road is where a large fruit and veg stall sets out ten tables piled high with fresh produce. The prices are dirt cheap and there are enough eager customers to keep six people busy until the market closes in the afternoon. As you proceed down Sclater Street things begin to get a little more organised compared with the chaos of Bethnal Green Road. Here you can find a dealer selling bike parts and a large stall specialising in DIY bits and pieces. Bargain hunters should look out for the archway shop selling good quality sheets and towels for just a few pounds with large cotton bath towels for just £3 and king size cotton sheets for only £4.

As you walk down Sclater Street the market opens up to the left to reveal an open square that serves as a car park during the week. The environment is a little messy, but there are signs that this part of the market is adapting to the growing prosperity of the area. The large meat lorry that used to set up here on a Sunday has gone and in its stead there is now an excellent French Deli trailer and another offering fresh bread and patisserie. There is even a stall selling Turkish delicacies such as baklava and fresh fetta. Ten years ago the only bread to be found here was *Mothers' Pride* and the choice of cheese would be Cheddar or Cheddar. The more healthy selection of food available here is only slightly marred by the hot dog van which fills the air with the smell of burnt onions and cheap meat.

One of the most popular features of the courtyard is the second-hand power tool dealer that spreads his stock on the floor for potential customers to examine. In the past the clothes sellers here were selling stuff in piles for £1 a garment, but now there are two well organised second-hand dealers offering a well displayed stock of jeans and casual wear for reasonable but not bargain prices. A fairly new arrival is the stationery stall offering a limited but cheap selection of notebooks, pens and other office essentials.

At the far end of this courtyard is Bacon Street that connects with Brick Lane. This street used to be a quiet backwater where dodgy old geezers sold dodgy old goods, but is now much busier with the opening of several lock-ups selling books, bric-à -brac, furniture and some very cheap kitchenware. There is now a vintage clothes store called *The Bacon Street Project* – a sure sign that this back street is destined to change in the next few years. Just opposite the square, on the other side of Sclater Street, is another large courtyard selling tools, electrical goods, computer games, kitchen pans and some suspiciously cheap bikes. The fruit and veg stall at the entrance to the courtyard is great value for the basics, and if you can hang around until the end of the day prices drop even further. " come on... I want to go home" exclaims the woman as she holds out large bags of bananas for £1.

Cheshire Street (from Brick Lane to Hare Marsh)

Cheshire Street has undergone something of a transformation in recent years and there are now a handful of smart shops including several vintage outlets at the beginning of the street. These new arrivals complement the variety and disorder of the stalls found here on a Sunday, which sell a mixture of new clothing, DIY equipment, second-hand books and further along a bewildering array of junk stalls. On the junction with Grimsby Street is a Brick Lane institution, *Blackman's Shoes*, which has been selling cheap shoes on the street for over a generation. The luxury flats that are being built on the right hand side mark the site of the old concrete warehouse that was once part of the market on a Sunday. It's not too much of a loss as the same stalls selling second-hand tools, used electronics, clothing, cameras, books, sheets and towels, kitchenware and collectables have moved to a similar warehouse further up the road which now marks the most easterly point of the market. The narrow alley next to Beyond Retro is one of the most established second-hand parts of the market and is a good place to look for all kinds of bric-à-brac from old lawn mowers to used hi-fi equipment. On a recent visit one of the old traders was offering four large outdoor Victorian lamps for just £20 and several gas camping lamps for just £5 each.

eastside bookshop

166 Brick Lane, E1 6RU
Tel: 020 7247 0216
Fax: 020 7377 6120
info@eastsidebooks.co.uk
www.eastsidebooks.co.uk
Open: Tues-Fri 11am-6pm,
Sat 11am-8pm, Sun 10am-7pm
Nearest tube: Liverpool St/
Aldgate East

Independent friendly bookshop in Brick Lane and a popular venue for author/book events, and writers workshops. Our stock includes fiction, travel, reference, children's books and we specialise in East London History.

Brick Lane
(from Bethnal Green Road to just beyond Cheshire Street)

Ironically, Brick Lane is one of the quietest and least interesting parts of Brick Lane Market. The junction with Sclater and Cheshire Street is busy with passing traffic and the few fruit and veg stalls in this area are always buzzing with the stall holders hollering their wares. The northern part of Brick Lane has fewer stalls but does have a good clothing stall selling High Street seconds at knock-down prices and a good junk shop which displays its wares on the pavement on fine days. The main attraction of this part of the market is the 24-hour Beigel Bakery which makes the freshest beigels in town.

South of the junction with Sclater and Cheshire Street, Brick Lane has changed with the removal of the bridge that once crossed the road and the closure of the second-hand outlets that traded from its arches. The permanent units have now been replaced by about 50 fly-pitches which now extend along this part of the market offering anything from CDs to second-hand clothes and watches. Brick Lane has a reputation for selling stolen bikes but the bike stall here is good value and totally legal – getting the bikes from auction rather than the black market. Further along on the right is a small junk shop selling anything from furniture to unusual things like a large floor sander that was recently found here for just £150. This part of the market now peters out but it is worth walking further to explore the two new indoor markets that are now a feature of Brick Lane.

Refreshment

There are lots of places to eat and drink on or around Brick Lane, the most famous place being the *Brick Lane Beigel Bakery*. The best coffee can be found at the two *Coffee @* cafés, one of which is near the beigel shop and the other at the southern end of the market at number 154. If you fancy a Sunday curry, further south on Brick Lane there is a huge selection of cheap curry houses.

Getting a Stall

There are many privately run lock-ups at Brick Lane that will rent space on a Sunday, it's best to have a look around and choose your site. For all other street stalls contact Tower Hamlets Central Market Office (see appendix).

Backyard Market
(next to the Atlantis Gallery and opposite the Vibe Bar)

www.sundayupmarket.co.uk
Open: Sat 11-6pm and Sun 10-5pm

This place is not difficult to find with several food stalls extending onto Brick Lane and funky music that can be heard from the street – played by the market's vinyl dealer who usually accompanies the tracks with a tambourine. This unprepossessing concrete warehouse is transformed at the weekend with about 80 stalls setting up here on a Sunday – the market is now the first on Brick Lane to start trading on a Saturday. On offer is a mix of independent designer clothes and gifts as well as several good value retro stalls. There is a far more arty and fashionable atmosphere here than at the more traditional parts of Brick Lane with dealers often attempting to sell original work and taking some care about the display of their wares. One stall offered a well chosen selection of vintage clothing, accessories and homeware and even had a website (www.myvintagestuff.com). Other interesting stalls included a Korean designer selling her contemporary garments for around £40 and another that offered a range of original T-shirts for £15 each. Among the retro clothing dealers there are some good bargains with several discounted rails offering garments reduced to clear for just £5. Hillary has been selling retro garments at Portobello on a Saturday for over 30 years, but is now also a regular here on a Sunday – offering bargains like jeans for £10 and a selection of cashmere jumpers for just £15. One of my favourite stalls belonged to the collective of Japanese artists that were selling their own range of funny and sinister cards, postcards and jewellery for just a couple of pounds. The cappuccino stall at the front of the market is a good place to go for a caffeine boost if you need it. After desperately searching for some originality in Camden in recent weeks it is great to find so many interesting things at this new addition to Brick Lane.

Local Attractions

Brick Lane Market has always been a good destination for bargain shopping with lots of unusual junk shops in the area. The main places to look are the second-hand lock-ups on Bacon Street - referred to in the main text. There are also lots of fashionable stores springing-up along Cheshire Street.

If Brick Lane has not exhausted you there are quite a few other markets within walking distance, including Spitalfields, Columbia Road and Petticoat Lane – all of which are open on a Sunday.

The Sunday Upmarket
(The Old Truman Brewery, entrances on Brick Lane, Hanbury Street and Wilkes Street)
www.sundayupmarket.co.uk

This vast indoor market has been at the heart of Brick Lane's transformation in recent years with the formerly empty surrounding streets becoming shopping avenues with boutiques and cafés. The Sunday market itself occupies the Old Truman Brewery and holds about 150 stalls offering all kinds of arts and crafts, hand-made toys, new and retro clothing, jewellery, accessories, shoes and homewares. The stalls here are often organised and run with enthusiasm by the designers themselves who often have novelties like business cards and websites to promote their wares. One such stall is run by a company called *Bobby Dazzler* (www.theworldofbobbydazzler.co.uk) which offers a fantastic range of original soft toys from £10 and is often mobbed by excited youngsters with their parents in tow. Something to please the adults is the art collective with a really interesting selection of handmade prints and drawings. Those looking for some retro style will not be disappointed here with lots of stalls to check out including one specialising in all kinds of shoes, boots and bags for a modest £5-10. Another stall is run by two students who collect a vast array of vintage jewellery, most of which is priced at around £4. Another interesting stall makes all kinds of unusual and elaborate leather belts for £18-20. With so many good stalls attracting large crowds every Sunday, the Upmarket seems destined to go from strength to strength.

Refreshment
There are about 40 catering stalls at the Upmarket serving food from around the world. Outside the market on the corner of Dray Walk is *Café 1001* which is one of the most popular eateries in the area and a little further down Brick Lane is a branch of *Coffee@* which does the best cappuccino in the area.

Getting a Stall
The Sunday Upmarket and Backyard Market are privately run. Details about trading at the markets can be found on their website (www.sundayupmarket.co.uk), or by phoning 020 7770 6100.

The Old Truman Brewery is an involving, exciting and sociable place to find yourself. Whether it be to eat in its restaurants, drink and dance in its bars, catch live bands, shop in its boutiques, hunt out a bargain at its weekend markets, check out an art exhibition, or just hang out, there is something to suit everyone's taste.

020 7770 6001 / 6100
www.trumanbrewery.com
events@trumanbrewery.com

The Old Truman Brewery
91 Brick Lane
E1 6QL

Broadway Market

London Fields, E8

www.broadwaymarket.co.uk
Rail: London Fields
Open: Saturday 9am-4pm

There have been a few sad tales to tell about the decline in London's street markets in the course of researching this new edition, so it is heart warming to report a market that has transformed itself into a vibrant success story in the last few years. Broadway market was one of the original chartered open markets and a thoroughfare for cattle grazed on nearby London Fields on its way to slaughter in Brick Lane or Smithfields. The post war years witnessed the decline in the market and by the 1990s it had dwindled to just a few stalls with the local council making occasional attempts to start a Saturday flower market which never got established. By 2004 Broadway market had ceased trading and it was not featured in the last edition of this book.

From this low point the last four years have seen the Tenants and Residents Association and Hackney Council work together to establish a quality food market on Saturdays which has gone from strength to strength and now incorporates much more than food. Over 60 stalls now show up here on a Saturday offering all kinds of things from fruit and veg to designer clothing and even one stall specialising in guitars, vinyl and posters. Broadway is not a farmers' market but does have many stalls offering delicious food with several traders selling fine cheeses and salamis and a wide choice of freshly made cakes, pastries and bread. There are a few specialist traders here, one just selling their own brand of chutneys with lots of different flavours and the chance to try before you buy and another offering their own selection of smoked meats. Carnivores will not be disappointed here with *Downlands Pork Butchers* and *Longwood Farm Organic Meat* both regulars among the many other specialist butchers to be found at the market. The organic fruit and veg stall offers all kinds of odd shaped produce at a price you would expect, but there is also an old-school fruit and veg dealer who is much better value.

The best thing about Broadway Market is the variety of things for sale with not only an excellent choice of food but also lots of unusual craft and second-hand gear. There is an excellent haberdashers stall with all kinds of things to attract the eye of children with an interest in crafts, from beads to colourful ribbons. The bike stall is run by the local bike man who can arrange to fix or service your two wheeled friend and also sells reasonably priced parts and tools. Further down the market there are lots of designers selling their wares including *Stiched*, who sell their exclusive range of designs here on a Saturday and at Greenwich covered market on a Sunday. One of my favourite stalls is the one specialising in very expensive (around £12), but very fine, hand-bound note books which make really unusual gifts. The market ends at the junction with Jackman Street, but the best is saved until last, because it is here that the markets vintage clothing stall can be found with lots of rails to sift through and bargains to be found on the discounted rails with a choice of garments for just £2.

Visiting the Broadway Market on a sunny Saturday it is heart warming to see so many people and stalls crammed into such a small road. These days a number of fly-pitches show up at the northern end of the market at the entrance to London Fields. The traders are a friendly bunch and only add to the appeal of the market with their selection of books, CDs and DVDs spread out on the pavement for just a few pence. They are a throw back to when this area was run-down and poor and are a welcome diversion if you are on your way to London Fields to enjoy a take-away lunch.

Broadway Market

Refreshment

There are many good cafés on Broadway Market including the *Gossip Café* and the excellent *La Bouche* as well as the large Spanish restaurant, *Solché Cilician*, at the far end of the market. My favourite is a branch of *F.Cooke* which has been serving pie and mash here long before the trendy haircuts arrived. There are several popular pubs on the market including *The Lamb & Mutton* and *The Dove*. There are lots of take-away stalls on the market including the Indian food stall which sells delicious samosas.

Local Attractions

Broadway Market has really taken off as a shopping destination in recent years with several very good vintage and retro furniture stores including *Broadway Retro* at number 16 which has interesting furniture and other collectables. *The Broadway Bookshop* is a great independent book store. London Fields is at the far end of the market and is a great place for a picnic on summer days and has a new lido for those who fancy a swim.

Getting a Stall

Those interested in a stall at the market can phone 0770 9311 869 or contact the organisers via the market's website (www. broadwaymarket.co.uk).

Chrisp Street

Market Square, Chrisp Street, E14
DLR: All Saints
Open: Monday-Saturday 9.30am-4pm (busiest Saturday)

This market pre-dates the rather ugly post-war architecture that now surrounds it. In 1994 the council built a futuristic new metal, concrete and glass roof for the market, which helps keep the rain off and is about the most attractive structure in the area. Suspended from the roof are large posters showing the market in its Victorian heyday, but far from being a celebration of the market's past, these old photographs only highlight its decline, particularly on a weekday when just a few stalls set up here.

The best day for a visit is a Saturday when the full complement of stalls offers a reasonable selection of bargain clothing for men, women and children, fruit and veg, fabric and haberdashery, shoes and cheap foodstuffs. Among the traders worthy of mention is the women's fashion stall with skirts made from contemporary fabric designs for just £7.99, and the shoe stall offering fashionable kids' trainers for just £8. Given the poverty and racial tension in this part of London it was heartening to see the addition of several Asian traders at the market and a fruit and veg stall that stocks a good selection of things like white aloo, long kudo and fresh curry leaves. As well as itinerant traders there are about twenty permanent lock-ups extending the range of clothing, shoes and household goods.

Getting a Stall
For further details contact Tower Hamlets Central Markets Office (see appendix)

Columbia Road

Columbia Road

Columbia Road east of Ravenscroft Street to Barnet Grove
Shops and a several courtyards on Ezra Street, E2

Tube: Old Street (Northern), Bethnal Green (Central)
Open: Sunday 8am-1.30pm

Columbia Road flower market is a real Sunday institution and its appeal seems to extend to those who have no interest in gardening and just go for the gift shops that run the length of the market and to relax at one of the many coffee shops and eateries that have sprung up around the street. I would recommend approaching the market from Ravenscroft Street and working your way to the eastern end where some of the best cafés are to be found. The market is easy to find from whichever direction you approach it – just walk in the opposite direction to those weighed down with bedding plants, cut flowers and large potted plants. On a busy Sunday morning the streets around the market can often resemble a scene from *Day of the Triffids*, with punters making slow progress as they shamble along, obscured by the massive plants they are trying to get home.

As you approach Ravenscroft Street there are several gift shops catering for the smart crowd that visit here every Sunday. Among the best shops in this part of the market are *Pot Luck* which sells simple, inexpensive white crockery and *The Pot Centre* which offers a great range of terracotta pots at very competitive prices – huge pots can be bought here for under a fiver. It's a good idea to wait until the end of your visit before buying these bulky bargains —thus avoiding the inconvenience of lugging them around for the duration of your visit.

The stalls selling cheap cut flowers at the junction with Ravenscroft Street mark the start of the market proper, and always have an enticing selection of flowers at well below the prices at your local florist. Here you can get a huge and varied spray for under a tenner and if you don't find what you want look out for the stall at the junction with Ezra Street which has a particularly extensive array of flora, but at slightly higher prices. Although the cut flowers remain a constant, most of the rest of the market varies its stock depending on the season. In the spring it is awash with trays of bedding plants for as little as £4 a tray, and lots of larger plants that will give the urban garden an instant splash of colour. As summer turns to autumn evergreens begin to dominate with greenery like lemon-scented goldcrest for £4 a plant (3 plants for £10) and statuesque eucalyptus plants for only £2. Large, mature plants can also be found here at well below nursery prices, such as six foot high palms for £15 and orange trees (bearing small fruit) for £20 - the latter reduced to £15 as the market neared its close. During the festive season Columbia Road is a great place to come for Christmas trees of all sizes as well as holly, ivy and other festive greenery and in recent years the market shops have opened in the evenings running up to Christmas for gift shopping.

The central avenue of the market is always a scrum with hundreds of people pushing their way along, often carrying armfuls of plants. If you get tired of the crush, try weaving between the stalls onto the pavement and taking a look at some of the shops that now line the street. There are lots of good gift, furniture, toy and hat shops to check out and in the middle of the market is the excellent *Lee's Sea Food* for a fishy treat. Towards the eastern end of the market are some of the best stalls for herbs with healthy looking pots of thyme, rosemary and sage all for around £1 a plant.

Columbia Road Market is not restricted to Columbia Road, but extends onto Ezra Street and several courtyards connected to it. The main courtyard is just off the junction and has several smart shops including Milagros selling a great selection of Mexican glassware, tiles and gifts. Further along there are several more courtyards one of which sells great value potted plants and shrubs. The neighbouring courtyard is now given over to second-hand stalls with a good selection of books, clothing and bric-à-brac to sift through and usually a few larger items of furniture.

Refreshment

There are numerous places on and around Columbia Road to get refreshment. *Lee's Sea Food* sells delicious fried calamari and giant prawns with a wedge of lemon and is highly recommended. *Café Columbia* also makes good pit-stop if you want to sit down and catch your breath. At the far end of Columbia Road are *The Laxeiro Tapas Bar* and, further along, *The Globe Organic Café* which are both safe bets. They have now been joined by a trendy coffee bar called *Treacle* which serves an expert cappuccino. *The Royal Oak* is a popular pub and its courtyard on Ezra Street has now been converted into a coffee stall, which rivals the more established coffee shop on the pedestrian walkway a little further along.

Local Attractions

Columbia Road is only 10 minutes walk from Brick Lane Market (see page 176) and further on is Spitalfields Market (see page 211). A few minutes walk in the other direction, on the junction of Goldsmith's Row, is *Hackney City Farm* which is great fun for the kids and has a wonderful café.

Getting a Stall

For further details contact Tower Hamlets Central Markets Office (see appendix)

Kingsland Waste

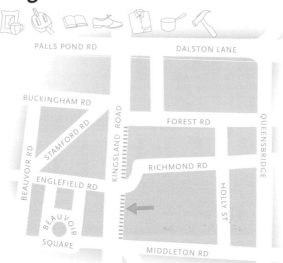

Kingsland Road between Forest and Middleton Road, E8

Rail: Dalston Kingsland
Open: Saturday 8am-2pm

For six days of the week this part of Kingsland Road is a rather unremarkable row of shops, but on Saturdays it is given over to about thirty stalls offering new and used goods and extending over about a quarter of a mile of wide pavement and parking space. There are some smart areas in this part of town, but this market does not attempt to cater to the well-heeled and has kept true to its working-class origins. If you like your markets clean, tidy and genteel then Kingsland Waste is probably not for you. But for those who enjoy looking for bargains in an authentic and rather seedy East End market it's well worth a visit.

The market is intersected by the busy Richmond Road. It is at this junction heading south that you usually find the carpet man who sells a reasonable selection of carpets and linos at low prices from his van. Continuing south, this part of the market is dominated by second-hand stalls selling all kinds of bric-à-brac, kitchenware, bikes and bike parts, books and occasional items of clothing. The woman who sells a selection of household goods like vases, glasses and cutlery is a regular feature at the market, helped by her young son who is in it for the pocket money. It was here that I recently acquired a very nice Chinese lacquer box for just £3. Nearby there is a ramshackle collection of stalls which

Kingsland Waste

deal with larger items like old lawnmowers, hi-fi's and televisions. The service is brisk and very little attempt is made to display the stock, with customers rummaging among the miscellany laid out on the pavement in search of a bargain. One budding DIY practitioner bought a large Bosch drill for just £15, while another picked out an assortment of good quality bike parts for just £8. There is now just one trader in the entire market selling new clothes but he has not let the monopoly go to his head – prices are very low with T-shirts for just £2, cotton shirts for just £3 and lots of trousers for under a tenner. At one of the better organised stalls an elderly lady offers all kinds of videos from kids' stuff like *Rosie and Jim* to a selection of Hitchcock classics.

My favourite stall is run by Norman Palmer who has been selling an interesting assortment of books, paintings, tools and household goods at Kingsland Waste for nearly thirty years. On a recent visit there were some wonderful old photographs for just 50p each and an attractive 1920s seascape in a large gilt frame for just £25. Nothing is priced and Norman is kept busy answering people's questions while also chatting with the regular visitors to the stall. A large stall dedicated to new DIY equipment lies further on and marks the end of this part of the market. Despite the changes Norman remains upbeat, 'It used to be a lot busier here, but this market still has a lot of potential'.

Further north beyond the junction with Richmond Road the market has changed noticeably in recent years. There is still the stall selling cheap stationary and its neighbour offering small DIY items like nails, screws, bolts and cables, but the stalls selling new shoes, clothing and household goods have moved on. The rest of the market is now dedicated to second-hand goods with about five regular second-hand stalls here offering all kinds of electronic goods, used kid's toys, videos, jewellery, phones and small items of furniture. These stalls have been joined in recent years by a small community of fly pitches that bring the market to a ramshackle and chaotic end long before the junction with Forest Road.

Kingsland Waste is a great place to visit on a Saturday morning and is a particularly important part of the East End, now that the massive Hackney Wick car boot sale has been closed to make way for the 2012 Olympics. The market still appears to be thriving as a flea market and this is perhaps the direction in which it is heading if the council have the good sense not to get too heavily involved

Refreshment

There is not very much refreshment to be found on the market and a tea and snack van is the only thing on the market itself. The best restaurant in the area is *Faulkners* at 424 Kingland Road for traditional fish and chips. *Kingsland Café* is also very popular for an artery clogging fry-up, although it is often difficult to get a seat on market days.

Local Attractions

The *Geffrye Museum* is about a mile further south along Kingsland Road and is well worth a visit for its unique display of English domestic interiors through the centuries.

Getting a Stall

For further details contact Hackney Council (see appendix).

Petticoat Lane

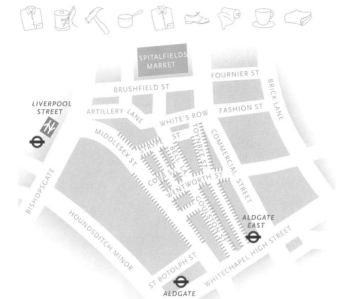

Middlesex Street, Wentworth Street (and adjacent streets), E1

Tube: Aldgate (Metropolitan, Circle),
Aldgate East (District, Hammersmith & City),
Liverpool Street (Circle, Central, Hammersmith & City, Metropolitan)
Rail: Liverpool Street
Open: All streets Sunday 9am-2pm,
Wentworth Street only Monday-Friday 10am-2.30pm
(shops, fruit and veg and a reduced amount of clothing and general stalls)

One of the most confusing aspects of visiting Petticoat Lane Market is the absence of any street by that name. Petticoat Lane was the former name for the main thoroughfare of the market, but it was renamed Middlesex Street in 1830. It is strange that the name of the market has remained in use, but it is appropriate given that the area has always been a place for the sale of clothing. Petticoat Lane is still one of London's most famous street markets, although it is now rivalled by more tourist orientated markets such as Brick Lane and Spitalfields which are both within walking distance.

£2.99
2 FOR £5

£5

♥
WORLD
PEACE

Petticoat Lane

Despite the competition, Petticoat Lane is still impressively big and busy on a Sunday, when thousands of people flock to the market from Liverpool Street Station to buy a cheap outfit or just soak up the atmosphere. The streets are lined with hundreds of stalls, concentrating mainly on new clothing, shoes and accessories. Just the sheer amount of people selling shirts or ties is enough to send you into option paralysis. Piles of cheap, cellophaned cotton, acrylic and silk garments seem to be the product of some mass breeding programme, as at each turn more cut-price bargains block your path. Price-busting multi-packs of knickers, socks and boxer shorts are everywhere, and there is a massive volume of ladies dresses and separates also available. Although most of the clothing is either purely functional or bandwagon street fashion, there are enough well-made and stylish garments to make a trip here worthwhile. One stall to look out for is the specialist in French Connection seconds and end-of-lines on Wentworth Street, which is popular on a Sunday and is also a feature of Roman Road Market on a Saturday.

At times Petticoat Lane resembles the rag market of Victorian times with stalls selling crumpled nylon clothing in large piles for just £1 an item and an ever changing flow of the East End's poor sifting through the piles for a bargain. Many of the traders call out for business with one shouting 'So cheap you'll buy it for someone you don't like', while another just hollowed 'cheap, cheap, cheap…' like a demented canary. A slightly more organised stall displayed its clothes on rails with everything marked at £3 including a selection of last season's *Top Shop* trousers which were attracting a small crowd of interested bargain hunters.

There is more to the market than just clothing however, with quite a few toy stalls selling cheap and tacky plastic stuff for the kids with the occasional quality item showing up here if you're lucky. As with everything at Petticoat Lane it's a matter of looking around. Petticoat Lane is a good place to find cheap luggage and bags with lots of stalls offering bargains like large suitcases with wheels for just £20 and reasonable quality rucksacks for just £8. The trader selling large cotton beach towels for just £7 and plain white Egyptian cotton throws for only £25 was also good value. In addition, there are always one or two decent shoe stalls offering fashionable and cheap footwear with one offering a good selection of seasonal throwaways for just £5-10.

If you're after a leather jacket visit the undercover area at the Aldgate end of Middlesex Street, known as *The Designer Market* where you could save serious money on leather jackets and coats. There are lots of different styles hanging on the walls, and the amount of individual traders with similar stock means productive haggling is an option.

Petticoat Lane is also well known for the international textile shops, which sell everything from African wax prints to Indian sari fabric. At prices starting from around £10 for four yards you can easily afford to do some fairly dramatic curtain-swagging or make yourself a sumptuous dress or skirt. The Middlesex Road end of the market is also a magnet for demonstrators – the people whose job it is to flog us the fragile hope that our lives will be better if we can shred, shine or sharpen something five seconds quicker. Few can resist the power of the patter. *Mr Euro-Tool*, *Mr Shine-Wipe* or *Mr Borner V-Slicer* are performers in the old tradition, so watch, admire and learn. The evangelists at the Liverpool Station end of Middlesex Street might not have such funky props, but the sales message is just as heartfelt: their energetic sing-songs are now a market staple on a Sunday.

Although Sundays is the main day for Petticoat Lane, there is a much smaller weekday market that caters for the locals with a limited selection of clothing, fruit and veg and other staples. The weekday market is a shadow of the Sunday event and only occupies a small part of Wentworth Street.

Refreshment

Petticoat Lane Market extends down a number of streets, so there are plenty of places to eat as you go round. *41 Bakery Café* is on the corner of Commercial Street and is the best place to get a cappuccino in the area. *Vernasca's* on Wentworth Street is an established favourite for traditional British grub, while *Happy Days* on Goulston Street has been serving quality fish and chips for years. If you don't mind eating on the move there are a number of fast food stalls on the market.

Getting a Stall

For further details contact Tower Hamlets Central Market Office (see appendix).

Boys & Girls COATS &
PUFFER JACKETS
DRESSES & SUITS

JOE BLOGGS   PO
PEPPERMINT   FLY
ZIP-ZAP TOUGH
LITTLE DARLING

0171-377-5

AFRICAN
LACE

AG

Petticoat Lane

Queen's Market

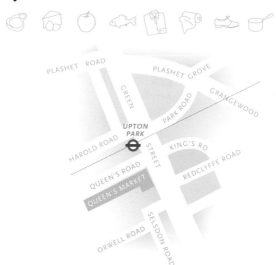

Green Street, South of Upton Park Station, next to Queen's Road, E13

Tube: Upton Park (Metropolitan, District)
Open: Tuesday and Thursday-Saturday 9am-5pm

Queen's Market has a long history dating back to Victoria's reign but in the sixties the market was moved to this purpose-built square and in 1979 a low roof was built over it. Thirty years later the place looks squalid and run–down, with little light penetrating beyond the entrance. Despite these badly-planned changes to the market, it is still thriving and even on a wet Tuesday morning crowds mill around the hundred or so stalls in search of bargains.

One of the reasons this market is still doing well is the large Asian and African communities in Upton Park who still prefer the hustle and bustle of a market to the antiseptic atmosphere of a supermarket. The market is good value for fruit and veg with lots of stalls competing for your custom and plenty of bargains if you are prepared to shop around. Queen's is also a great place to find Asian and African produce, with many specialist food outlets offering things like Dasheen leaves and bunches of fresh Pak Choi. The handful of fresh fish stalls have a varied range of catches and are good value with staples like smoked haddock alongside more exotic things like conger eel and octopus. In addition there are several butchers on site offering all manner of bloody bargains as well as a stall selling farm-fresh eggs.

Queen's Market is also the place for cheap fabric with lots of stalls offering colourful and plain material (including African and Asian designs) with prices starting from £1 per metre. If sewing isn't your thing, there are stalls selling cheap and cheerful clothing, including one specialising in bargain footwear. Although many of the consumer durables here are of limited appeal, the stall selling large kitchenware is excellent value with a good choice of stainless steel pans.

The market is currently under threat of development which will involve the market moving onto Green Street while the site is demolished and replaced with smart flats and a new market area. The plans are not popular with some of the markets' traders who are valiantly campaigning against the current plans, see their website for further details (www.friendsofqueensmarket.org.uk).

Refreshment

Queen's has a few caffs within the market area including *Halal Pride* and *Ozzey's Café*. Just outside the market – facing Green Street – is the long established *Queen's Fish Bar*.

Getting a Stall

For further details contact Newham Council (see appendix).

Ridley Road

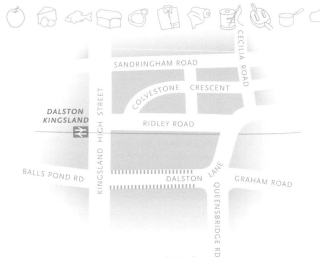

Ridley Road, between Kingsland High Street and St Mark's Rise, E8

Rail: Dalston Kingsland, Hackney Downs
Open: Monday-Saturday 9am-5pm

Ridley Road is one of North London's biggest markets, with attitude to match. Running the length of a street of lock-up shop units between Kingsland High Street and St Mark's Rise, this market is the place where locals from Dalston's diverse communities come to stock up on cheap food and essentials – even on a weekday it's buzzing. The Afro-Caribbean influence in both Dalston and its market is particularly strong, and not only in terms of the massive selection of unusual food products. As the crowds of people increase towards midday, the lively – and occasionally slightly abrasive – atmosphere is stoked by shops blasting out reggae and groups of traders and shoppers stopping mid-flow to shoot the breeze.

Although Ridley Road is by no means just a food market, the extensive selection of both fresh and preserved produce is probably the magnet drawing most shoppers. Further down towards St Mark's Rise goods become increasingly alien, with tropical standards like mango, cassava and sweet potato joined by baskets and trestles piled with unfamiliar leaves, vegetables, meat and fish, and lurid drinks like 'Sky Juice' on sale by the glass. The sheer number of rival stalls and shops means you are spoilt for bargains, with each trader offering something at a discount price such as boxes of mango for just £3 and three bunches of Coriander for just £1. Ridley Road is a great place to get a week's fresh produce for under a tenner and many visitors leave the market weighed down with more shopping than they should sensibly carry. Staples like lentils, oil, nuts and flour are all very cheap but sold in large bags that make a strong back, or trolley, essential.

In addition, the substantial local Turkish community means that there are plenty of Mediterranean vegetables on offer, with good prices on key ingredients like lemons (6 for £1) and continental parsley (60p a bunch). There is also a huge Turkish food shop on the junction with St Mark's Rise that is ideal for all the other Mediterranean foodstuffs you can't find on the market. More conventional produce is also well-stocked, featuring prices like 6 large oranges for £1 and a large bag of ripe bananas for the same amount. Most street markets these days do not have a fish stall, Ridley Road has several, selling anything from British stalwarts like cod and haddock, to more unusual species like shark and huge conga eels. At one fish stall the crabs were still struggling in vain to escape their fate.

There are a few drawbacks to Ridley Road and one is that it can get very busy, with the narrow gap between stalls clogged with people trying to move in every direction at once. When this happens, traders get a bit shirty if you're not buying courgettes for ten, and might talk you into buying more than you want. Stand firm if you just want a pound of spuds. The squeamish will also find Ridley Road difficult to cope with as it is peppered with stalls selling meat and fish products which bear little resemblance to the innocuous vacuum-packed portions in Tesco's: turkey gizzards, saltfish, goat stomachs, cows' and pigs' feet are all piled up, picked over and chopped up in full view.

Food is definitely the thing at Ridley Road, but there are plenty of other goods on offer, with standard market clobber (electricals, cheap and brand-name clothes and shoes, bedding, underwear, cosmetics and hair accessories) dotted throughout, and a smattering of textile units and stalls selling haberdashery and vivid materials like African wax prints, sequined voiles and rainbow selections of satin, cotton and acrylic mixes. One stall dealing in electrical goods had a large selection of boxed, brand-name phones for just £5, while another trader offered a great choice of leather bags and belts for £7. The best clothing stall was at the far end of the market where three shaven headed East Enders sold branded sports and casual wear in large disordered piles. The men made no effort to sell the goods and simply said " seven pounds" to every question asked of them.

Ridley Road

Refreshment

Len's Café (half-way down on the left) is secreted underneath the lock-ups for an almost subterranean cup of tea. For something more exotic, try one of the several kebab take-aways that make kebabs good enough to eat when sober. *Ridley Bagel Bakery* has been re-branded as *Mr Bagel*, loosing much of its character in the process. At 41 Kingsland High Street, *Shanghai* serves dim sum throughout the day in a listed interior that used to belong to the area's famous pie and mash shop.

Local Attractions

The *Rio Cinema* is just a few minutes walk north of the market on Kingland High Street. The Cinema is one of the best independents in the Capital and often has matinee performances

Getting a Stall

For further details contact Hackney Council (see appendix).

Roman Road

Roman Road from St Stephen's Road to Parnell Road, E3

Tube: Mile End (Central, Metropolitan and District)
Open: Tuesday, Thursday and Saturday 8.30am-4.30pm

Roman Road and its market are a strange mix of the cosmopolitan and the parochial. Approaching the market along Roman Road you will pass a photography gallery, an art gallery, several smart designer clothes shops and even a Buddhist Centre, and yet by the time you reach the market it feels as though you are in the heart of the East End. Most of the people who shop here are locals and one of the stall-holders spoke of the other side of Victoria Park as though it were some distant and exotic land. The area does have the occasional rough pub and some poor housing, but the market itself is a surprisingly friendly and pleasant place to shop and a great place to find discounted high street fashion. Visitors to the area should take the opportunity to explore Victoria Park and the Grand Union Canal which are just 5 minutes walk from the market.

Roman Road is one of London's longest roads with the market occupying the far eastern end beginning at the junction with St Stephen's Road. The mysterious stall that sells women's garments one at a time from a box is still going strong. The pitch is always surrounded with eager local women waiting for the next item in the hope that it will be in a style they like and in a size that fits them – price is never a problem as most items are sold for just a few pounds. On a recent visit a large Jamaican woman had selected a bin bag full of clothes which were patiently counted out and priced for between £1 and £3 – the whole bag of clothes amounting to £45. There are other more conventional clothing stalls along this part of the market with lots of basic street fashion for around a £10. One trader specialises in ex-catalogue women's clothing for a fraction of the original price while another stall brands itself as *Punkyfish* and sold bright teenage fashion at well below Camden and Brick Lane prices.

Among the stand out bargains is the stall selling fashionable shoes for around £20 a pair and another dealing in all kinds of bags from nylon rucksacks for as little as £8 to a stylish leather travel bag for only £45. One of the best stalls for women's fashion can be found near Ewart Place and offers M&S ladies fashion at a considerable discount.

It is at this point in the market, between Libra Road and Hewison Street, that most of the fruit and veg stalls are located. The fruit and veg is good quality but, unlike Ridley Road, there is not much of a cultural mix here and the selection of produce is fairly monotonous. To compensate for the culinary uniformity of the market there are several music stalls specialising in soul and contemporary R&B and playing their music as an accompaniment to the hectic shopping. One of the busiest stalls on Roman Road is the one selling accessories, which is usually surrounded by women and girls sifting through the hairbands, clips and plastic jewellery – with most items priced at 20p and a few larger items of jewellery for £2.

The eastern end of the market is the most interesting for discounted clothing with several stalls specialising in slight seconds and end-of-line garments from leading designers and High Street chains. The stall on the junction with Usher Road is long established and has hundreds of French Connection seconds for a fraction of the usual price. The discounts vary depending on the garment with a pair of FCUK jeans requiring an easy repair for only £4 while a colourful v-neck jumper with no obvious fault was £15 instead of the usual price of around £60.

Roman Road Market is still a great place to spend a morning, but there are a few glum faces along the street and more than a dozen empty shops along the market. One trader bemoaned the market's decline and blamed it on a change in public shopping patterns: "...people used to come from all over the place to shop here. Now they want to shop in places like Blue Water." Another trader was less philosophical about the situation, instead resorting to laconic asides to punters. One old geezer gave the man some comfort, "what have you got to complain about, you're young, you like doing-up old cars and of course there's always a bit of the other...mind you, interest in that goes in the end." And with that he was off down Roman Road.

Roman Road

Refreshment

The long established *L. Randolfi* caff has sadly closed but there are still some good places to get refreshment along the market. The best cappuccino on the street can be found at *Franco's Coffee Bar* on the corner of Gladstone Place with the Café inside the *Idea Store* just opposite coming a close second. If you fancy some traditional Cockney fare you could try the eel, pie and mash shop, *G.Kelly* or walk to the *Saucy Kipper* at the end of the market for a fish and chip take-away supper.

Local Attractions

The Idea Store situated on Gladeston Place, just off Roman Road, is a fantastic new type of library. It offers CDs, DVDs and internet access as well as books and even has a coffee shop. On fine days it's well worth making the journey down St Stephen's Road to explore the Grand Union Canal and Victoria Park.

Getting a Stall

The market is run by Tower Hamlets Council (see appendix).

Old Spitalfields Market

Commercial Street
London E1
020 7247 8556

Nearest Tubes
Liverpool St/Aldgate
Open
Thursday
Antiques & Vintage
Friday
Fashion, Arts & Crafts
Sunday
The Full Market

Portobello Green Market

'Under the Westway'
Portobello Road
London W10
0800 358 3434

Nearest Tubes
LadbrokeGrove/
Notting Hill Gate
Open
Friday
Fashion & Vintage
Saturday
The Full Market
Sunday
Bric-a-Brac

SPITALFIELDS
ANTIQUE MARKET
Commercial Street, London E1
EVERY THURSDAY from 7am

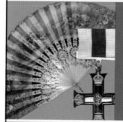

COVENT GARDEN
ANTIQUE MARKET
**The Jubilee Hall, Southampton St
Covent Garden WC2**
EVERY MONDAY from 6am

Tel: 020 7240 7405
Sherman & Waterman Associates

Spitalfields

Commercial Street between Folgate and Brushfield Street, E1

Tube: Liverpool Street (Central, Metro & Circle lines)
Open: Thursday 7am-3pm (antiques and collectables and a Crafts market),
Friday 10am-5pm (crafts market)
Sunday 10am-5pm (Main Sunday Market including Crafts)

Looking at the main entrance to Spitalfields Market on Commercial Street there seems little evidence that the place has undergone a major redevelopment taking over four years to complete and costing many millions. The magnificent Hawkesmoore church which stands opposite was built in 1729 and adds to the impression that things have remained unchanged. It is only when you look up to see the imposing Norman Foster-designed glass office block, behind the traditional market, that some idea of the changes becomes apparent.

Inside the market the transformation is everywhere to see. The peeling wrought iron columns have been stripped and painted grey. The roof has been renovated and cleaned to let more daylight into the building. Vast industrial-sized lamps project light onto the ceiling and add to the bright feel of the place. Even the dirty tarmac that once dominated the interior has been replaced by tasteful stone effect flooring. The quirky and rather tatty style of the old market has been replaced by a modern reworking of a Victorian building. Looking through the market you can see where the old market has been demolished and a new glass roofed shopping area created with lots of sandstone, steel and glass in evidence.

The market has continued despite all the upheaval and quite a few of the old stall holders – including Tom, who sells a fine selection of men's retro shirts – are still going strong. The booksellers continue to be an important part of the market, offering good quality fiction for £2 a copy. The number of good bread and pastry stalls has increased in recent years and there is now a cheese and deli stall with lots of delicious cheeses available to taste. The market has its fare share of interesting bric-à-brac stalls with one trader turning his table into an elaborate edifice of antique rugs, pictures and mirrors. There are a few bargains to be found at the market despite the smart environment, with one retro clothing stall selling all trousers for £10 and dresses and jackets for only £20. One of the most original stalls specialised in vintage eyewear (www.klasik.org) with lots of classic frames and a prescription lens service. They were even offering a few bargains with an unusual pair of 60s sunglasses reduced to only £10.

Further through the market, as the building becomes more modern, the stalls change with the emphasis on new goods and lots of stalls offering independent designer clothing and accessories. One young trader (www.lovefromhettyanddave.co.uk) sells a funky selection of hand-made jewellery and proudly displays a magazine cover showing Amy Winehouse wearing some of her creations. Stylish women's fashion is particularly well represented with *Tatty Brown* (www.tattybrown. com) offering a range of hand-made dresses for £25-55 and attracting a small crowd of interested shoppers. Men don't have as much choice but there are still some interesting things to find here including one trader selling fabulous *Seamus Jones* shirts made from Liberty prints for £55. Not all the clothes on sale at the market are hand-made and original designs, but even the imported gear with anonymous labels was of good quality.

It is at this stage that the open market area ends and the stylish shopping avenues extend in the direction of the new glass bank that stands at the western end of the complex. The shops here are all up-market boutiques and expensive eateries, but some space has been allocated for artists to display and sell their works from white cubicles.

Spitalfields Market is a wonderful place to visit on a Sunday when it is at its busiest and most exciting, but there is also a smaller market on Thursday and Friday and there are plans for a Saturday market.

Getting a Stall

The Thursday antiques market is managed by a separate company (see below), but for all other parts of the market phone 020 7247 8556 for further details.

Spitalfields

Spitalfields

The Antiques and Collectables Market

Open: Thursday 7am-3pm

About 100 stalls show up here every Thursday selling anything from bric-à-brac and retro clothing, to collectables and fine antiques. Spitalfields has kept enough of its old character to make it an ideal setting for such a market and with the decline in stall space at Camden Passage (see page 56) and Bermondsey still yet to find its feet after redevelopment (see page 130), the Thursday market could possibly be the largest of its kind in London.

The market has a good mix of things from small items for £5 to large elm chests for £400 and even a Rolex for several thousand pounds. Clothing varies from odd assortments of cheap retro gear to exclusive designer wear. One specialist stall is called *Famous France* (www.famousfrance.com) and deals exclusively in French jewellery, clothing and accessories from names like Christian Dior and Givenchy. There are some really unusual things to be found here like the stall offering examples of the taxidermist's art with lots of woodland creatures captured forever in animated poses.

Spitalfields has several good bookstalls on a Thursday with plenty of paperback fiction and one trader specialising in manuscripts. George has been selling his well-polished selection of collectable hand tools here for the last two years after many years at Camden Passage. He likes the market and takes real pride in the display of his stock. George and his fellow traders have transformed Spitalfields into the best collectables markets in London and they are greatly helped by the venue which is light and airy and yet protected from the elements.

Getting a Stall

The Thursday market is run by *Sherman Waterman Associates Ltd* who can be reached on 020 7240 7405.

Refreshments

There are lots of smart cafés and restaurants within the market these days with the *Daily Grind* now established in the corner of the old market near Commercial Street. The smarter, more fashionable dinning places tend to be located further back in the market with branches of *Giraffe*, *Canteen* and *Leon*.

Local Attractions

The main attractions are the other Sunday markets in the area. Petticoat Lane (see page 197), and Brick Lane (see page 176) are both within easy walking distance of Spitalfields.

Walthamstow Market

Walthamstow

Walthamstow High Street, E17

Tube/Rail: Walthamstow Central (Victoria)
Open: Monday-Saturday 9am-5pm

Many locals claim that this is the longest market in Britain, which is probably an exaggeration given the size of Portobello Market (see page 106), but it is certainly quite a trek from St James Street to the end of the market at Hoe Street. Many local markets are now facing difficulties with the rise of the supermarkets, but Walthamstow is a rare and wonderful exception. There are many reasons for Walthamstow's continued success, among them the fact that the wide thoroughfare of Walthamstow High Street has been pedestrianised, making it a natural focal point – as well as a great place for shopping and strolling. The shops in the area complement the market rather than compete with it, with some excellent butchers, fishmongers and continental food retailers.

There are about 500 stalls lining the half mile route of the market selling all manner of things. Cheap shoe stalls abound with one of the best situated towards the Hoe Street end of the market selling fashionable women's shoes for between £5 and £25. Another shoe stall offered slight seconds of men's shoes for just a tenner, which included some fashionable suede shoes that appeared in good nick. Although the clothing is not as trendy as that found at Camden Market, there are plenty of stalls selling street fashion at keen prices, such as the one flogging overstocks and slight seconds from High Street shops like

River Island, Monsoon and *Evans* for £5 a garment. Another trader had simple cotton jackets with the Gap label for only £10, rather than the £40 charged on the High Street. Among the many fabric stalls on the market, there's a particularly good one on the junction with Palmerston Road, offering quality curtain fabric for as little as £3.99 per metre. Another stall, further along, sells Asian and African fabrics at very low prices. Walthamstow is also a good market to visit for kitchenware and household goods with large aluminium pans for just £10 and bargains like 5 bars of soap for £1 and 36 toilet rolls for just £3.99.

There are some superb fruit and veg stalls with one selling carrier bags of seedless grapes for only £1 and another offering 2lb of best vine tomatoes for the same price. Walthamstow used to have a very limited range of fruit and veg, but there has been an increase in diversity in recent years and what you can't find on the market can always be found at other food stores along the route. Likewise, the *H. Clare* stall has been selling quality fresh fish here for umpteen years, but only the basics, for more exotic fish try the fishmongers opposite.

Unusual stalls at Walthamstow Market include the tape and CD stall which offers a massive selection of tapes for just £1 each. Music on tape is becoming a thing of the past, but some people have a cassette player in their car and for a few quid they can add to their in-car music collection. Another quirky feature of the market is *Bev's Homemade Cakes* which sells colourfully decorated cakes for £2-£2.40, with all cakes guaranteed free from artificial flavourings and small samples for those who want to try before they buy. The market also has two stalls where the name of *Dyson* is mud, trading as they do in Hoover bags and accessories. For romantics who would rather return to their loved one with flowers than vacuum cleaner accessories, there are several stalls selling cut flowers and one dealing in cheap bedding plants. Among the good deals were large pots of heather or brightly coloured coreoposis for just £2 a pot.

Walthamstow High Street is an ideal place to visit if you want to see a neighbourhood market still in its prime. Unlike many local markets it's busy even on a weekday – although Saturday is the best day to go. A good way to approach the market is through the wonderful Springfield Park and Walthamstow Nature Reserve, which will take about 45 minutes, but gives you a soothing dose of nature before the hustle and bustle of the market.

Refreshment

Among the best places to find good British food on the market is *Copperfield Snack Bar* (at the top end near Hoe Street), as well as *Bunters' Grill* and *First Stop Café* (in the middle part of the market). *L.Manze* pie and mash shop is an established favourite, while *Café Rio* is a more recent, but equally popular café with seating outside on fine days. If you don't mind eating on the move there are lots of food stalls on the market including *Seth's Spice Hut* for Indian snacks and *The Old Tea Bag*, which despite the name serves a decent cuppa.

Local Attractions

Walthamstow High Street has some interesting shops along its route with many charity shops including the largest *Oxfam* shop in the Capital at the Blackhorse Road end of the market. There is also a great range of fabric shops on the High Street and some excellent food shops which, combined with the market, make this a great place to shop on a weekend.

Getting a Stall

For further details contact Trading Standards Office, 8 Buxton Road, Walthamstow E17, Tel: 020 8520 4071.

Well Street

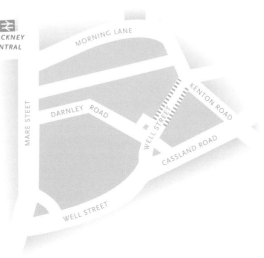

Well Street from Morning Lane to Valentine Road, E9

Rail: Hackney Downs (Liverpool Street),
Hackney Central (Broad Street)
Open: Monday-Saturday 9.30am-4pm

The founder of *Tesco* supermarket, Jack Cohen, had a stall here over seventy years ago, so it's only fitting that the *Tesco* store at the top end of the market takes most of the local trade today. These days there are only a few if any stalls here during the week and just a handful on Saturdays. The fruit and veg stall is a long established and good one, but stands alone with just a few stalls selling cheap clothing at the top of the street. The quality butchers and two good charity shops make this an interesting street, but one not worth venturing too far to visit.

Getting a Stall
For further details contact Hackney Council (see appendix).

Whitechapel

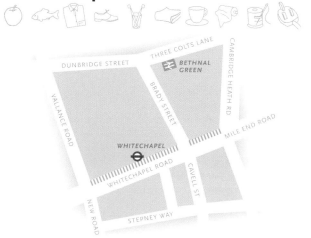

North side of Whitechapel, from Vallance Rd to Brady St, E1

Tube: Whitechapel (Metropolitan, District)
Open: Monday-Saturday 8.30am-5.30pm, Thursday 8.30am-1pm

Whitechapel market has a long history dating back to the 17th century. The street is one of the widest in London because of its importance as a thoroughfare for cattle on their way to Smithfield Market and Whitechapel Market developed as a last trading post on the journey. In Victorian times most of the traders were Irish and Jewish immigrants to the East End. Both communities have now largely left the area and their place has been taken by a new wave of immigrants from the Indian subcontinent. Thankfully, the Bengali and Bangladeshi communities enjoy shopping at market and, while some East End markets are struggling, Whitechapel is still a bustling place with over sixty stalls setting up here, even on a weekday.

Whitechapel has always been a home to the poor and although the prosperity of the City is now encroaching on the area, the market is still a place where price and value for money are paramount. The fabric stalls are all very cheap with lots of material for just £1 per metre and plenty of unusual designs and patterns to choose from. Most of the clothing stalls offer generic street fashion at very low prices, but there are always a few good bargains to be found, such as the women's cotton slacks for just £10 and the colourful summer dresses reduced to only £8. Likewise, most of the shoes available are basic street wear, but one stall specialised in trainers and had some reasonable styles for £20 a pair. The most unusual traders are the two fish men who both have stalls selling huge frozen fish from large freezers placed on the pavement. The fish are packaged and bear names such as *Rohn* and *Bual* and do not look appetising for those unfamiliar with them. It might be better to stick to the fresh mackerel and haddock which are also available.

Whitechapel also has stalls selling small electrical goods, haberdashery, bags, kids' clothes and toys, and a trader selling good value kitchen equipment; but the market really excels when it comes to fresh fruit and veg. There is a wealth of choice to be found here extending from the basics to more exotic things like fresh curry leaves and bitter gourd. On a recent visit there were bargains such as three large bunches of coriander for just £1 and boxes of ripe mangoes reduced to just £2. If you're looking for difficult to find ingredients for a curry there is no better market to visit.

Whitechapel Market is a place were all kinds of cultures and races mix and where London's culture is displayed in all its complexity. At one stall a burley turban wearing Sikh trader was talking to a friend in the broadest cockney accent while at another stall a Bangladeshi trader could speak hardly any English and seemed an exotic import from another world. These people are carrying on a market tradition that has deep roots in London's history and long may they continue to thrive.

Refreshment
Whitechapel High Street does have a few rather dodgy pubs, but is poorly served for cafés and restaurants. *Peckish?* is a small sandwich bar which does a reasonable coffee. For good cheap Indian food it might be better to try some of the places on Brick Lane – just ten minutes walk from the market.

Local Attractions
The main cultural landmark in this part of town is the *Whitechapel Gallery* which displays modern art and has the added appeal of a great coffee shop. *The Idea Store* is a new kind of library at the eastern end of the market, which is a popular resource for the local population and is well worth a visit. *KVJ* is just a few doors down from *Whitechapel Gallery* and is the cheapest place in town for batteries, blank CDs, ink cartridges, and other essentials.

Getting a Stall
For further details contact Tower Hamlets Council (see appendix).

Whitechapel Market

SARAH GREEN'S
ORGANICS

The Hall Farm Shop,
North Street,
Tillingham, CM0 7ST

Farmers' Market

The concept of Farmers' Markets, where local food producers sell direct to the public, has been one of America's more benign imports. In the last ten years this type of market has proved a great success in London, providing a lifeline for many small independent farmers that were struggling to survive. *London's Farmers' Markets* was the pioneer in the field and is still the most important organisation, applying strict rules to ensure that only genuine farmers – no food distributors – sell at their markets. A later arrival on the scene is *City & Country Farmers' Markets*, which has helped to revive some failing local markets such as Hammersmith.

Both organisations have their own listings below, but special attention has been given to the *Growing Communities Market* in Stoke Newington, which is a thriving independent and one of the best market experiences you can find in London.

London Farmers' Markets

Webite: www.lfm.org.uk
E-mail: info@lfm.org.uk

The London Farmers' Market in Pimlico is a good example of what you can expect from these events. The market takes place in a small, tree shaded square in one of the smarter parts of Pimlico with a statue of the young Mozart looking down upon the activity that involves about twenty stalls every Saturday morning. There are quite a few stalls offering seasonal vegetables with unusual things like Swiss chard and pumpkin among the more usual British vegetables including some sturdy looking celery stalks – very different from the anaemic examples you find in the supermarket. At one stall a Norfolk farmer was selling honey from his 250 hives for £3.25 a jar. He was very keen to discuss his farm and was enthusiastic about the markets that have provided a valuable source of income for him – he now spends the weekend in London and also trades at Blackheath Market on a Sunday.

The *Manor Farm* stall sells all kinds of food products made from their own livestock including four large venison burgers for a very reasonable £3.50. Another meat stall at the other end of the market was offering even better value with things like six farm-produced sausages for £2.50 and large packs of cooked ham for only £3. There is always a good choice of cheese at the market with several producers showing up to sell cheese made with care on their own farms. The fresh fish stalls are equally impressive with varieties like monkfish and wild sea bass on display.

One of the best stalls was that run by *Chegworth Valley Farm* which sold a great range of apple juices for £3 per bottle as well as strawberries for £1.50 per punnet and several varieties of apples. At this stall you could choose the juice with different varieties of apple producing different levels of sweetness. The only consistent thing is the freshness of the product. Other stalls included several very good bread and cake sellers, a flower stall with produce from the traders' own market garden and one selling lavender and lavender products with strongly scented lavender soap for £5 a bar.

The Pimlico market is typical of the Farmers' Market experience, although not all the venues have the same charm as Pimlico Square. What all the markets share is good value produce and a belief in properly produced food. Visiting a *London Farmers' Market* is a great experience not only for the great food you can find there, but also for the chance to see that rare thing – British farmers with smiles on their faces.

Acton W3
Public Square on
Acton High St, King Street
Tube: Acton Town or
Ealing Common
Open: Saturday 9am-1pm

Blackheath SE3
Blackheath Rail Station Car Park,
2 Blackheath Village
Rail: Blackheath
Open: Sunday 10am-2pm

Clapham SW4
Bonneville Primary School,
Bonneville Gardens
Tube: Clapham South
Open: Sunday 10am-2pm

Ealing W13
Leeland Road, West Ealing
Tube: Ealing Broadway (then bus)
Open: Saturday 9am-1pm

Islington N1
William Tyndale School (Behind
the Town Hall), Upper Street
Tube: Angel
Open: Sunday 10am-2pm

Marylebone W1
Cramer Street Car Park,
Corner Moxon Street
(off Marylebone High Street)
Tube: Baker Street
Open: Sunday 10am-2pm

Notting Hill W8
Car Park behind Waterstones
(access via Kensington Place)
Tube: Notting Hill
Open: Saturday 9am-1pm

Pimlico Road SW1
Orange Square, Corner of Pimlico
Road & Ebury Street
Tube: Sloane Square
Open: Saturday 9am-1pm

Queen's Park NW6
Salusbury Primary School,
Salusbury Road
Tube: Queen's Park or
Bondesbury Park
Open: Sunday 10am-2pm

South Kensington SW7
Bute Street, Kensington
Tube: South Kensington
Open: Saturday 9am-1pm

Swiss Cottage NW3
Eaton Avenue off Finchley Road
Tube: Swiss Cottage
Open: Wednesday 10am-4pm

Twickenham TW1
Holly Road Car Park,
Holly Road (off King Street)
Rail: Twickenham
Open: Saturday 9am-1pm

Walthamstow E17
Town Square by Selbourne
Walk Shopping Centre,
Off the High Street
Open: Sunday 10am-2pm

Wimbledon SW19
Wimbledon Park First School,
Havana Road
Tube: Wimbledon Park
Open: Saturday 9am-1pm

City & Country Farmers' Markets

Tel: 01689 860 840
Tel: 07780 520 610
www.cityandcountryfarmersmarkets.com
chris@cityandcountryfarmersmarkets.com

This organisation has done a great deal to bring farmers' markets to London. Some of the markets only visit a site once a month, but popular markets like the one held at the Oval have now become weekly fixtures. The website is an excellent resource with information about the future market dates.

Alexandra Palace
Muswell Hill
Bottom Entrance, N8
Open: Sun 10am-3pm
When this venue is unavailable,
the market will be held at:
Campsbourne School
Campsbourne School,
Nightingale Lane,
Off Priory Road, N8.

Dulwich
Dulwich College,
Dulwich Common, SE21
4th Sunday of the month
9am-1pm

Manor House Gardens
Manor House Gardens,
Old Road, Lee, SE12
1st Saturday of the month
10am-3pm

Hilly Fields
Hilly Fields,
Hilly Fields Crescent,
Brockley, SE4
2nd Saturday of the month
10am-3pm

Telegraph Hill
Telegraph Hill,
Telegraph Hill Park,
Erlanger Road, SE14 5LS
3rd Saturday of the month
10am-3pm

Hammersmith
Hammersmith,
Lyric Square, King Street, W6
Every Thursday 10am-3pm

The Oval
The Oval, St Mark's Church,
Kennington Park Road, SE11
Every Saturday 10am-3pm

St George Wharf
The Riverside Walk,
Vauxhall Bridge, SW8
3rd Thursday of the Month
10am-3pm

Woodcote Green
Woodcote Green Nurseries,
Woodmansterne Lane,
Wallington, Surrey, SM6
3rd Saturday of the month
10am-4pm

Caterham on the Hill
The Green, Guards Avenue,
Caterham on the Hill, Surrey, CR3
4th Sunday of the month
10am-3pm

Eltham
Passey Place,
Off Eltham High Street, SE9
3rd Sunday of the month
10am-3pm

Deptford
Deptford Park,
Evelyn Street, SE14
4th Sunday of every month
10am-3pm

Stoke Newington Farmers' Market, (Growing Communities)

William Patten School
Stoke Newington Church Street, N16
www.growingcommunities.org
Rail: Stoke Newington
Open: Saturday 10am-2.30pm

This market has been supplying organic and locally produced food to the citizens of Hackney since 2004. The event is run by Growing Communities – a Hackney-based organisation who promote local farmers and sustainable food production. The organisation also runs a vegetable box scheme supplying produce from its own urban gardens and makes effort to insure that the food sold at the market is both locally produced (within about 150 miles from London) and 100% organic.

The application of all these principles might sound a bit worthy and pious, but the market that fills the playground of William Patten School every Saturday is a lot of fun. When I last visited they were giving away cake to celebrate the market's anniversary and there was a free knitting class for youngsters making their first forays into the world of wool.

About twenty stalls set up here on a Saturday, but the diversity and quality of the produce mean that there is a lot to see, taste and buy and enough excitement to draw a large crowd. The Suffolk farmers called *Muck & Magic* had reasonably priced, organically reared, lamb, pork and beef. Another stall offered a limited but fresh choice of fish caught from their own boat and the neighbouring stall offered a range of cheeses from *High Alham Farm*. *The Celtic Bakers* had a large display of organic breads and pastries while a more modest stall sold farm fresh eggs and honey from their Essex small holding. There were several traders selling organic fruit and veg with *Sarah Green's Organics* making a real effort to display their seasonal produce. Visitors are spoilt for choice for take-away food with Indian, Turkish and Creole snacks and wonderful cakes for those with a sweet tooth. The organisers have thoughtfully provided a large seating area so people can enjoy their food in comfort and perhaps get a shot of caffeine from the busy coffee stall.

Leaving the market after a delicious snack and with a bag full of fresh organic produce, it's not difficult to see why this place has become a permanent and much loved part of Stoke Newington life.

Getting a Stall

Contact Growing Communities on 020 7502 7588

Peckham Farmers' Market

Peckham Square, Peckham High St, SE15
Rail: Peckham Rye or Queens Road
Open: Sunday 9.30am-1.30pm
Annette annettecauneen@tiscali.co.uk
07951 464 732

This farmers' market was initially managed by *London Farmers' Markets*, but is now run independently. The quality of the food is still very high with all the bread, eggs, meat, fish and fruit and veg you would expect from a good farmers' market.

Car Boot Sales

North

Holloway, N7
Seven Sisters Rd (behind McDonalds) and opposite Odeon Holloway
Saturdays 8am-4pm,
Sundays 10am-2.30pm
100 pitches
Tel: 01992 717198

Kilburn, NW6
St Augustine's School,
Kilburn Park Road
Saturdays 11am-4pm (set up 8am)
100 pitches
Tel: 020 8440 0170

Nightingale School, Bounds Green Rd
Bounds Green, Tottenham, N22
Sundays 7am-1pm (6am set up)
250 pitches
Contact: Giant Boot Sales
Tel: 020 8365 3000

Bounds Green School
Bounds Green, Tottenham, N22
Sunday 12noon-5pm and
Bank Holiday Mondays
Contact: Giant Boot Sales
Tel: 020 8365 3000

Tottenham, N17
Tottenham Community Sports Centre,
Tottenham High Road
Thursdays from 9am-2pm
55 pitches
Contact: Countryside Promotions
Tel: 01992 468 619
www.countrysidepromotions.co.uk

Wood Green, N22
New River Sports Centre,
White Hart Lane
Fridays from 6am-2pm
60 pitches
Contact: Countryside Promotions
Tel: 01992 468619
www.countrysidepromotions.co.uk

West

Chiswick, W4
Chiswick Community School,
Burlington Lane
First Sunday of month (except Jan),
8am-1pm (set up from 7am)
200 pitches
Tel: 020 8747 0031

South

Battersea , SW8
New Covent Garden Market,
Nine Elms Lane, Battersea
Sundays 8am-2.30pm (set up
6am)
250 pitches
Tel: 0151 233 2165

Battersea Technology Centre, SW8
Battersea Park Road
Every Sunday 1.30pm-5pm
Tel: 07941 383 588

Brixton, SE5
Coldharbour Lane
Every Sunday 7am-1pm
Tel: 020 7701 4291

Meridian Sports Club, SE7
Meridian Sports Club,
Charlton Lane
Saturdays from 7am-12noon
150-200 pitches
Tel: 020 8856 1923

Wimbledon Stadium, SW17
Plough Lane, Wimbledon
Wednesday 9am-2pm, Saturdays
7am-2pm
Tel: 020 7240 7405

East

William Morris School, E17
Foley Lane, Billet Road,
Walthamstow
Sundays from 6am
Tel: 07932 919 707

Out of Town

Bishop Stortford, CM23
Bishop Stortford Town Centre,
Sundays from 7am
130 pitches
Contact: Countryside Promotions
Tel: 01992 468 619
www.countrysidepromotions.co.uk

Flamingo Park, BR7
Flamingo Park (A20),
Sidcup, Kent
Sundays (April-Aug) 9.30am-3pm
pitches: 300
Tel: 020 8309 1012

Harlow, CM19
Pinnacles Industrial Estate,
Harlow, Essex
Sundays from 10.30am
320 pitches
Contact: Countryside Promotions
Tel: 01992 468 619
www.countrysidepromotions.co.uk

Hatfield, AL10

Birchwood Sports Centre, Longmead,
Hatfield, Herts
A1, Junction 4, then follow signs
Sundays from 10.30am
320 pitches
Contact: Countryside Promotions
Tel: 01992 468 619
www.countrysidepromotions.co.uk

Hayes, UB3

Hayes & Yeading FC,
Church Road, Middlesex
Every Wednesday & Friday
8am-2pm (set up 7am)
70 pitches
Tel: 020 8573 2075

Hounslow, TW3

Hounslow West Station Car Park,
Middlesex
Saturday 7.30am-2pm (set up 7am)
Sunday 7.30am-2pm (set up 7am)
75-150 pitches
Contact: Bray Associates
Tel: 01895 639912

Middlesex Showground, UB8

Park Road, Uxbridge
Every Sundays 7am-1pm
300 pitches
Tel: 020 8561 4517

North Weald, CM16

From M11 junction 7, take A414 Road
to North Weald, Essex
near Talbot round about
Saturdays 10.30am-2pm
150 pitches
Contact: Countryside Promotions
Tel: 01992 468 619
www.countrysidepromotions.co.uk

Sheppherton, TW17

New Road, Shepperton, Surrey
Saturdays 7.30am-2pm
Tel: 07807 609 283
www.sheppertoncarboot.co.uk

Waltham Abbey, EN9

Upshire Road, Waltham Abbey,
Essex
M25, Junction 26,
then follow signs to Upshire
Sundays from 10.30am
475 pitches
Contact: Countryside Promotions
Tel: 01992 468 619
www.countrysidepromotions.co.uk

Wanstead Rugby Club, IG8

Wanstead Rugby Club
Roding Lane North,
off Woodford Avenue
Buckhurst Hill, Wanstead, Essex
Saturdays from 7am-1.30pm
(June- mid September)
Tel: 01279 871 117
Country Group

Chigwell Rise, IG8

Chigwell, Essex
(nr Davis Lloyd Center)
Sat 7am-1.30pm (April-May)
Tel: 01279 871 117
Country Group

Boreham
Generals Farm, CM3

Main Road Boreham
Chelmsford
Sat 7am –1.30pm
-(July-mid Septenber)
Tel: 01279 871 117
Country Group

The Continental & French Markets

Paras Bristiel French Markets

wwwpborganisation.com
Tel: 01233 812 223

Lyric Square, Hammersmith
Meridian Square, Stratford
Devonshire Square (not far from
Liverpool Street Station)
Ealing Green
Croydon North End
Bexley Heath
Chelmsford
Didcot
Newbury
Aylesbury
Camberley
Hitchin

Paras Bristiel run regular continental markets throughout the south east with quite a few events taking place in the London area. The markets are well organised with orderly displays of fresh produce and all goods protected from the elements with large white canopies. The events are a welcome addition to the market scene and are well worth a visit, with 20–30 stalls setting up on each trading day. Visitors can expect to find food and other goods from across the continent with fresh bread, cheeses, biscuits and prepared meats all strongly featured.

Brunomart

www.brunomart.com
Tel: 01737 832 718

Greenwich,
Cutty Sark Gardens, SE10

Walthamstow,
The Town Square, E17

Sutton, High Street, Surrey, SM1
Croydon, North End, CR0

This organisation runs French markets consisting of about 20 traders that offer an authentic range of French foods, clothing, accessories and gifts. The markets sporadically visit London at four main locations and are worth tracking down for their excellent French cheeses and prepared meats, fresh bread and patisserie. The biscuit stall is always popular offering about 20 types of French biscuit. If food isn't your primary concern the markets also have excellent leather bags, stylish summer dresses and even contemporary colourful watches.

The Brunomart timetable of events is published on their website so log on to find out about their future schedule.

Brunomart in Walthamstow

The Week at a Glance

	M	T	W	T	F	S	S
CENTRAL LONDON							
Berwick Street & Rupert Street	●	●	●	●	●	●	
Cabbages and Frocks						●	
Charing Cross Collectors' Fair						●	
Covent Garden	❶	④	④	④	④	④	④
Earlham Street	●	●	●	●	●	●	
Leadenhall	●	●	●	●	●		
Leather Lane	L	L	L	L	L		
Lower Marsh	L	L	L	L	L	▼	
Piccadilly Market		❶	④	④	④	④	
Smithfield	✪	✪	✪	✪	✪		
Southbank Book Market	❷	❷	❷	❷	❷	❷	❷
Strutton Ground	L	L	L	L	L		
Tachbrook Street		●	●	●	●	▼	
Whitecross Street	L	L	L	L	L		
NORTH LONDON							
Alfie's Antiques Market		●	●	●	●	●	
Camden	▼	▼	▼	▼	▼	●	●
Camden Passage			❶	❷		❶	
Chalton Street					L		
Chapel Market		●	●	●	●	●	●
Church Street		●	●	●	●	●	
Hampstead Community Market						●	●
Hoxton Street	▼	▼	▼	▼	▼		
Inverness Street	●	●	●	●	●	●	
Kilburn Square	●	●	●	●	●	●	
Nag's Head	●	●	❶	●	●		❸
Queen's Crescent				▲		●	
Swiss Cottage			▼		●	●	
Wembley Sunday Market							▲
Willesden			●			●	
WEST LONDON							
Bayswater Road & Piccadilly						▼	●
Hammersmith Road			●	●	●	●	
North End Road	●	●	●	▲	●	●	
Portobello	▼	▼	▼	▲	▼	●	▼
Shepherd's Bush	●	●	●	▲	●	●	

SOUTHWEST LONDON	M	T	W	T	F	S	S
Battersea High Street						●	
Brixton Market	●	●	●	●	●	●	
Broadway and Tooting	●	●	▲	●	●	●	
Hildreth Street	●	●	▲	●	●	●	
Merton Abbey Mills						●	●
Nine Elms Sunday Market							▲
Northcote Road	▼	▼	▲	▼	●	●	
Wimbledon Stadium							▲

SOUTHEAST LONDON	M	T	W	T	F	S	S
Bermondsey					✪		
Borough Market				▼	▼	●	
Choumert Road & Rye Lane	●	●	●	●	●	●	
Deptford Market			●		●	●	
East Street		●	●	●	●	●	●
Elephant & Castle	●	●	●	●	●	●	
Greenwich Market			▼	❶	▼	●	●
Lewisham High Street	●	●	●	●	●	●	
North Cross Road						●	
Southwark Park Road	●	●	●	●	●	●	
Westmoreland Road							❸
Woolwich Market		●	●	▲	●	●	

EAST LONDON	M	T	W	T	F	S	S
Bethnal Green Road	●	●	●	▲	●	●	
Billingsgate		✪	✪	✪	✪	✪	
Brick Lane						▼	●
Broadway Market						●	
Chrisp Street	●	●	●	●	●	●	
Columbia Road							▲
Kingsland Waste						●	
Petticoat Lane	▼	▼	▼	▼	▼		▲
Queen's Market		●		●	●	●	
Ridley Road	●	●	●	●	●	●	
Roman Road		●		●		●	
Spitalfields				❶	▼	▼	●
Walthamstow	●	●	●	●	●	●	
Well Street	●	●	●	●	●	●🖉	
Whitechapel	●	●	●	▲	●	●	

KEY

● Open all day
▲ Open half-day
L Lunch time markets
▼ Market partially open

✪ Open early mornings only
❶ Antiques Market
❷ Book Market
❸ Bric-à-brac
❹ Arts & Crafts

Appendix

Listed below are all the relevant council addresses if you're interested in trading at a council run market:

Camden Council
Environmental Department,
Consumer Protection Services,
Camden Town Hall,
Argyle Street,
WC1H 8NL
Tel: 020 7974 6917

Greenwich Council
Public Services,
11th Floor Riverside House,
Woolwich High Street,
SE18 6DN
Tel: 020 8921 5835

London Borough of Hackney
Environment Directorate,
Dorothy Hodgkin House,
12 Reading Lane,
E8 1HJ
Tel: 020 8356 3367

London Borough of Hammersmith and Fulham
Environmental Protection Division,
Town Hall Extension,
5th Floor, King Street,
W6 9JU
Tel: 020 8753 1081

Islington Council
Public Protection Department,
159 Upper Street,
N1 1RE
Tel: 020 7527 3830

Kensington and Chelsea Council
Market Office,
72 Tavistock Road,
W11 1AN
Tel: 020 7727 7684

Lambeth Council
Market Trading,
53 Brixton Station Road,
SW9 8PQ
Tel: 020 7926 2530

Lewisham Council
Wearside Service Centre,
Wearside Road, Lewisham,
SE13 7EZ
Tel: 020 8314 2050

Newham Council
Property & Design Department,
City Gate House,
246-50 Romford Road,
Forrest Gate,
E7 9HZ
Tel: 020 8430 5760

Southwark Council
Markets Department,
SAST House,
Dawes Street,
SE17 1EL
Tel: 020 7525 6000

Tower Hamlets
Market Service,
29 Commercial Street,
E1 6BD
Tel: 020 7 377 8963

Wandsworth Council
Markets Department,
Room 59, Town Hall,
Wandsworth High Street,
SW18 2PU
Tel: 020 8871 8546

Westminster City Council
Licensing Department,
33 Chester Street,
SW1X 7XD
Tel: 020 7641 7822

The National Market Trader's
Federation is a useful contact and
can arrange insurance for market
traders:

**The National Market Trader's
Federation**
Hampton House, Hawshaw Lane,
Hoyland, Barnsley,
South Yorkshire, S74 0HA
www.nmtf.co.uk
Tel: 01226 7490 211

Market Listing

Subject Index

Bikes

Books

Bric-à-brac

CDs/Tapes

Childrenswear

Clothes (New)

Clothes (Second-hand)

Crafts

Delicatessen / Organic Food

Index

Electrical Goods

Fabrics & Haberdashers

Fish

Flowers and Plants

Index

Jewellery and Watches

Meat

Shoes

Tools and Hardware

Toys

Videos/DVDs

Index

BLUE BIRD
SELECT
ASSORTMENT

HARRY VINCENT LTD. HUNNINGTON NEAR BIRMINGHAM.